Beyond Homelessness

Beyond

Frames of Reference

Benedict Giamo & Jeffrey Grunberg

PHOTOGRAPHS BY MEL ROSENTHAL

Homelessness

UNIVERSITY OF IOWA PRESS 🌵 IOWA CITY

University of Iowa Press,
Iowa City 52242
Text copyright © 1992 by
the University of Iowa Press
Photographs copyright © 1992
by Mel Rosenthal
All rights reserved
Printed in the United States
of America

Design by Richard Hendel

Library of Congress Cataloging-in-
Publication Data
Beyond homelessness: frames of reference/
    [edited] by Benedict Giamo and Jeffrey
    Grunberg; photographs by Mel
    Rosenthal.—1st ed.
        p.   cm.
    ISBN 0-87745-364-0 (alk. paper)
    1. Homelessness—United States.
    2. Interviews—United States.
    I. Giamo, Benedict.   II. Grunberg,
    Jeffrey.
    HV4505.B49   1992   91-42952
    362.5'0973—dc20   CIP

96 95 94 93 92 C   2 3 4 5 6
96 95 94 93 92 P 1 2 3 4 5 6

Toward a

better life for

each citizen among

us now homeless

and in memory of

Jerzy Kosinski

So it is that now I denounce and defend, or feel prepared to defend. I condemn and affirm, say no and say yes, say yes and say no. I denounce because though implicated and partially responsible, I have been hurt to the point of abysmal pain, hurt to the point of invisibility. And I defend because in spite of all I find that I love. . . . I sell you no phony forgiveness, I'm a desperate man—but too much of your life will be lost, its meaning lost, unless you approach it as much through love as through hate. So I approach it through division. So I denounce and I defend and I hate and I love.

—From the epilogue to Ralph Ellison's *Invisible Man*

CONTENTS

FOREWORD

From the beginning of this project in January 1990, our belief has been that, in order to confront homelessness, we needed to transcend popular culture's incessant monologue on the topic. Repeatedly, the public has been told that homelessness presents three problems, which serve as solutions as well: housing, housing, and housing. Such single-minded slogans, though having a very real basis in the lack of affordable, low-income housing in this country, have foreshortened our perception of the homeless and have stunted our conversation about their problems. This masking of homelessness shapes individual and social perceptions alike. It influences how we see the problem, how we name it, and how we respond to it. In effect, it blinds us to the relationship between homelessness and other pertinent problems of American society: the questions and issues related to social change, class divisions, racial inequities, poverty amid affluence, alienation, and personal crises in living.

Only by moving from a monologue to a dialogue will we be able to face some of these broader questions and issues. How effectively we deal with the problems of the homeless at this time in history will depend on just how well we recognize the frames of reference which we use to explain—and, at times, to explain away—homelessness. In the interest of going beyond such frameworks to sound out other voices, we have interviewed nine individuals who range across the humanities, social and medical sciences, and human services, all in an attempt to bring new ideas and outlooks into perspective and to challenge established misconceptions of the social problem. Such misconceptions, by the way, are apparent on both ends of the political spectrum. It is our hope that these conversations will stimulate debate on public policy and private initiative and lead to a more comprehensive sense of social reality and a reawakening of the moral imagination.

We were pleased and excited to get the cooperation of Robert Coles, Hazel Dukes, James Dumpson, Jerzy Kosinski, Robert Jay Lifton, Sister Mary Rose McGeady, Herbert Pardes, Robert Rieber, and Peter Rossi. Each of these individuals has been involved in investigating and writing about the problems of the homeless (and/or related social phenomena) or in directing organizations (both private and public) which aim toward helping the homeless.

As a collection of interviews, this book attempts to place the *experience* of homelessness (those very harsh conditions of uprootedness, estrangement, destitution, and disorder) within the broader *context* of American social life. In the process of exploring both experience and context, this book also tries to reveal what we make of such lives that we come into contact with and bear witness to. What do we make of all this—the conditions of the homeless so prevalent on the streets and in the shelters of our major cities today? What stories do we tell ourselves, and what stories do we propose to tell others? What approaches and methods and convictions are these stories based on? And how do the homeless, and society in general, benefit from the results of such activities?

Of course, such stories are not imaginary tales. They are grounded in the historical, social, and personal realities of people who are living *in extremis*. They also emerge from a variety of methods (historical and cultural analysis, demographic assessments, observation and interviewing, fieldwork, advocacy, psychiatric interventions, rehabilitative models, psycho-social interactions) and from simply following the drift of homelessness over time and place.

All of the people who appear in this collection have made use of one or more of these methods to inform and enrich their knowledge of homelessness. The stories they tell are very much a part of their "way in" to the situation of homelessness. These stories are also intimately related to their professional backgrounds and identities, to the work they have been involved in, and to who they are as individuals, as distinct personalities, deeply concerned about the relationship between the development of self and the development of society.

In light of Jerzy Kosinski's death during the course of this project, perhaps some thoughts and recollections are in order. We were surprised to hear from him early one morning. He had just returned from Europe and read through our book proposal and request for an interview. Evidently, something had struck a chord, for he phoned immediately. During our conversation, he spoke of his concern for the homeless (whose plight had preoccupied him for the past three years), his commitment to go ahead with the interview, and a "solution" he was getting ready to propose to the Jewish Presence Foundation, of which he was the president. All of this was said in a matter of minutes with an intense, passionate conviction. Six months after his call, after finally getting through his very protective secretarial entourage, we met with him in his New York City apartment and spent over two hours together in animated, provocative, amusing, and candid conversation.

His death six months later was a shock neither of us was ready for, a loss that continues to haunt us. He will be missed by all of us who have been so moved by his own childhood experience of homelessness during World War II, which figured so vividly in his first novel, *The Painted Bird*, and by his other fictional writings, which portray a more metaphysical homelessness—the struggles of self, detached and transient, always living in contention with a hostile, destructive world bent on diminishing the prospect of survival.

Yet there are moments that endure, for as Kosinski himself once put it: "In that moment of feeling fused with articulation, one's very life expands. You can buy and sell and rent everything but that moment." We chose the form of interviews, of conversations, because they tend to reflect such moments. Since the form of dialogue has an especially immediate, dynamic, and personal quality, we believed that this approach would spark spontaneous and interesting encounters. We could genuinely meet each other in an interaction of words and faces. We also hoped that this form would evoke new perspectives and the heightened sense of possibility that often accompanies such fresh outlooks. In the end, we were not disappointed.

In scope, the perspectives embodied in these interviews range along a continuum from highly systematic and socially structured outlooks (best represented by Rossi and Dumpson) to existential and phenomenological points of view (championed by Coles and Kosinski). All of the others fall somewhere in between: while Dukes and Pardes cluster toward Rossi and Dumpson, Lifton and McGeady seem to take a middle position, and Rieber leans toward Coles and Kosinski. Whereas the more systematic and structured positions tend to proceed from the assumptions of the social welfare state—critiquing policies and adverse social forces—the existential and phenomenological approaches tend to foreground the values of humanistic individualism. These are general tendencies (orientations, if you will) and should not be taken as rigid classifications of anyone's position on homelessness. For example, although a demographer and sociologist concerned with statistical evidence, Rossi is highly aware of and deeply concerned about the condition of individuals suffering on the streets. And although Coles and Kosinski start with the existential realities of the individual, each in his own way has documented the "aberrations" of social life, whether reflected in destructive racial attitudes or in the dangerous forces of the mass media.

In an attempt to organize these various interviews thematically, we have divided the book into three parts: "In the American Grain," "The Public Interest," and "The Shapes of Social Conflict." Occasionally, even within a given section, the perspectives may be set in sharp contrast to each other, as is the case with Rossi and Kosinski. Through their differences, these two observers express distinct traditions and approaches within American social thought. No doubt, within this range of lively discourse, the reader will find a good deal of such diversity, but also a good deal of common ground too. Rather than present a totalistic vision of homelessness, a repetitious nodding of heads throughout this collection, we hope that the book captures something of the democratic process itself—an open exchange of viewpoints, critiques, fears, and expectations for the future.

Democracy at work is both frustrating and invigorating. But the proof of its value is not only in the process; it is also in the results. We hope these interviews present the kind of fruitful friction that can move us beyond our present social crisis—a crisis that includes not only the condition of homelessness, but the state of the "homeless industry" and the plight of American society as well.

We would like to express our special gratitude to each of the contributors whose cooperation and generosity made this book possible. They took the time out of their hectic schedules to meet with us, welcomed us into their homes and offices, contended with not one but two interviewers, and put in the extra effort to review and make final changes in the edited transcripts. And they gave freely, with no concern for the fact that neither we nor the University of Iowa Press, which is nonprofit, could offer any money, stipend, or honorarium.

We would be remiss if we did not mention the inspiration and insights offered by Kenneth Burke, good friend and luminous mentor, who met with us before our first interview took place. He gave us an "exploratory" interview, a chance to try all this out on him, to test our mettle. When we arrived he was ready for us and shuffled into the kitchen, an extension of his study, like a great minister bent out of time. He had a hymnal in his hands and boisterously began singing, "Rock of Ages, cleft for me, / Let me hide myself in Thee." He went through all four stanzas and then looked up with a knowing smile, the great cerebral skeptic emerging from the faithful soul. "You want to know about homelessness?" he shouted. "I'll tell you about homelessness!" He went on, "It all began when the earth ceased to be the center of the universe." We were off and running . . .

We would also like to thank Mel Rosenthal for supplying the photographs that precede each interview. Rosenthal is a socially concerned photographer; his is not a hit-and-run approach. While photographing the homeless, he has stopped to build up his own frame of reference, listening to the stories of those he comes into contact with and talking to them of his own interests and concerns. We hope that these photographs will evoke the presence of homelessness, add to our conversations about them, and, in Rosenthal's own words, "Help make clear that the cause of the people who are now homeless is the cause of all human beings."

Additionally, we would like to thank Dan Biederman and Eri Noguchi (from the Grand Central Partnership), Carol and Craig Colby, and, from the University of Notre Dame, Teri Haus, Christopher Lane, Margaret O'Shaughnessy, and Sandra Wiegand for lending their assistance to the project. Finally, appreciation goes out to Alexandra Verna, Iris and Tommi Welch, Joel Hodson, Stuart Unger, Melissa Barry, James Waugh, Cynthia Scott, Ronald Dorris, Gilburt Loescher, Michelle and James Duane, and Jeanne and Robert Rodes for their support and encouragement during some trying times.

Part 1

In the American Grain

PETER H. ROSSI

Permanence and Change

BENEDICT GIAMO: In the preface to your book *Down and Out in America*, you mentioned that while you had been poor, you had never been extremely poor and homeless. To what extent did your experience of being poor influence your outlook on these problems?

PETER ROSSI: I am sure the experience does make a difference, but I don't know in which specific ways. I grew up in Queens, New York, out in the neighborhood called Corona. I was a kid during the depression and experienced how frightened all adults were that they would be the next victims of unemployment and deprivation. I was eight years old in 1929 at the start of the depression. So my whole childhood was haunted by the aura of economic insecurity and restricted aspirations. When the depression was over, in 1942, they took me into the army. I was in City College when I was drafted.

JEFFREY GRUNBERG: Were you studying sociology then?

ROSSI: Yes, I was going to be a social worker. I was profoundly influenced by a very gentle man by the name of Samuel Joseph, a sociology professor. I was a red, carmine, Marxist. Oh yes, a Trotskyite, as a matter of fact. Joseph taught a required sociology course. He made every student get up and make a little talk about social problems. So, I got up (in 1940 this was really chutzpa at City College) and talked about Marxism as the solution to the problem of anti-Semitism. When I finished Joseph said, "Rossi, sit down. Listen, Jews have enough trouble." So I sat down, crushed. He was an extremely gentle man; that was probably the most aggressive thing he had ever done to one of his students. After class, he said, "Come over here." And I went over and sat down and he said, "You know, you're pretty smart, but don't give me that horseshit." And then he asked, "What are you going to do for a living?" I said, "I don't know; maybe I will become an economist." He said to me, "Why don't you become a social worker? There are lots of jobs for Catholic social workers."

So I got interested in social work and I headed in that direction. I was hoping to get a civil service position in the public welfare department as a Social Investigator I, with a magnificent starting salary of $1,800 per year. Now, for that much money, you could live in the Village, buy a record player, and lead a modest but secure life; so that is what I was going to do.

GRUNBERG: And this decision had to do with what you thought the government was or was *not* doing?

ROSSI: The choice of a job was not a statement about the society. As a Marxist, I thought social work was a kind of inadequate bandage. But compared to alternative jobs, it was benign, secure, and respectable. Keep in mind that the depression was a situation in which the society was really stagnating with opportunities opening up mainly in the public sector. So we looked forward to see what sort of opportunities were available to us, and we looked primarily toward civil service.

Welfare work was a reasonable job, not very well paying but you could get into it on merit. All you had to do was pass their exams. Everything was closed off. Society was being shaken by World War II. All of us were kind of scared that the depression would come back again. It was meaningful work—working against the forces of society to reclaim and sustain its victims.

GIAMO: After the war, how did you get back in step with society? Did you pick up your studies?

ROSSI: I and others of my cohort were sucked into the explosion of academia. My friend Marty Lipset wrote to me while I was still in Germany, saying that I should go to graduate school because there were a lot of jobs opening up in academia. So when I got out of the army in 1945, I went to graduate school at Columbia to get my Ph.D. I got my degree in 1951. The opportunities that opened up postwar led to an explosion of aspirations for many in my college cohort.

GIAMO: Were you studying with Robert Merton at the time?

ROSSI: Well, he was there and I took his courses, but I worked mainly with Paul Lazarsfeld. He discovered that I had a talent in empirical research and encouraged me to develop and exercise those skills. It was Lazarsfeld who launched me on my academic and research careers.

GIAMO: Were you in the trenches when you received this letter in Germany?

ROSSI: (laughs) No, Lipset's letter arrived after May 8, VE Day, around the time when I was due to be discharged. I had to decide what to do with all my benefit eligibility. I had about four years of schooling coming to me under the GI Bill. The GI Bill benefits paid tuition and had an allowance for books and equipment. The GI Bill made it possible for me and many others in my cohort to go on to graduate school and to aspire higher than we had any thought about doing in the prewar period. A stipend came with it, about $50 per month, not enough for gracious living, but life in New York was very cheap: the rent for my apartment on 106th Street was $28.50 per month, utilities included.

GIAMO: What was it like for society to shift from depression to prosperity with the war coming in between? Did the change give you a different viewpoint, especially after coming back from the war?

ROSSI: Yes, opportunities developed that we did not have before. Before the war, we were mainly survivors, always looking for some kind of reasonable, steady niche to get into. But after the war, if you could turn into a risk-taker, there were many opportunities. Those who could not make the shift took safe jobs in secondary school teaching or in the social welfare bureaucracy. One of the big perceived risks was leaving New York City. Many of us said, "How could you leave New York?" In order to be able to take advantage of the opportunities, you had to think in terms of the national labor market, which meant that you had to consider Ohio, or maybe Illinois. Ironically, the armed forces took us all over the world but we were still provincial New Yorkers when discharged.

GIAMO: Looking back now, do you think you took the right risks?

ROSSI: Absolutely. No regrets. I could have entered a different field, most likely economics. I am envious of the economists. They seem to know more.

GRUNBERG: What do you mean: "They . . . know more"?

ROSSI: Well, they have theories about how things work. Economists say that people are motivated by incentives and they are deterred by penalties. So all you have to do is work out the proper schedule of benefits to accomplish social change.

GRUNBERG: B. F. Skinner?

ROSSI: Sort of, but on a very large scale. The major incentives for a corporation are the profits and, for people, wages and salaries. That is a very powerful theory. I think that the economic basis of homelessness is often forgotten in the morass of pathology that we see day to day. But there is no way that you can provide housing to people who cannot afford any rent. I think that this cry for affordable housing is a misleading slogan. Five million new housing units: if they charge $100 per month rent, none of the homeless could afford it. The homelessness problem is more an income problem than a housing problem.

GIAMO: How do you compare the knowledge that economists have with the knowledge that other social scientists produce? In terms of homelessness, is it good knowledge?

ROSSI: Well, it is hard to say if it is good knowledge. It certainly is more systematic and a little bit more structured in form than some of the other, more mushy ways.

GRUNBERG: There is some sort of antieconomist position that some social scientists seem to display.

ROSSI: Yes, money is not everything; therefore, money is nothing.

GRUNBERG: Perhaps economists offer a perspective that is too simple for the other social scientists to accept.

ROSSI: Yes, I know, but simplification helps. You just have to be careful that it doesn't take over the world. Those who see a bewildering complexity to life, well, that is the way it really is. But you can also be completely dazzled by complexity and you can say that everybody is very,

very different. Then everybody needs different strokes for different folks, and there are millions of strokes; so what can we do?

GIAMO: Sounds like the information on homelessness. How would you characterize the knowledge "out there" on homelessness?

ROSSI: There are some very clear messages available to us that are often not heard. People say that only 30 percent of the homeless can be characterized as being chronically mentally ill—only 30 percent. So that is supposed to mean that chronic mental illness is not a cause of homelessness. But the fact is that that proportion comes up pretty consistently, except for someone who studies people in a shelter for the chronically mentally ill and talks about all the homeless there being mentally ill. Well, of course. But the information is quite firm and robust and comes out in study after study. What it means is that mental illness among the homeless is magnitudes greater than in the general population.

The issue is not about the information, but about interpretations of the information and what lessons it has for social policy. There is a loose connection between descriptive information about a group like the homeless and the social policies that might be appropriate given that description. Okay, so as with chronic mental illness, there are at least a dozen social policies, ranging all the way from "put them back in the loony bin" to "assign a psychiatrist or a case manager for each one."

Case management is a real scam, a marvelous way to keep social workers from dealing with clients. All they do is deal with the "case" and talk to each other as to how to manage it.

GRUNBERG: There are disadvantages to oversimplification. This is what some people resent about certain advocate groups, such as the various coalitions for the homeless. Their work actually prevents people from understanding all that is homelessness—its sheer complexity. Have you worked with such advocate groups?

ROSSI: I really haven't had very much contact with them. The main problem I have had with the advocates is that they won't have any contact with me. First of all, the research that I did in Chicago [1985] was roundly denounced by the Chicago Coalition for the Homeless. You see,

I came up with 2,700 people who were homeless on an average night, and the advocates were talking about 15,000 to 20,000. The disparity between the two was just more than they could stand. I still remember this one lady, for example, possibly from Traveler's Aid, at a meeting where I gave a presentation on the results of the findings. She broke down into tears, saying, "What am I going to do about my program if there are only 2,700 people out there? You've got to be wrong."

GRUNBERG: Now there's an example of the economics of homelessness.

ROSSI: Well, there is a shelter industry out there. Around every social problem, an industry grows. It's fantastic, this capitalistic system, in its ability to supply whatever is needed, so long as there is money for it.

GIAMO: Nationwide, the estimates on the number of homeless today range from 350,000 to 3,000,000. What makes for such discrepancy, and where do you see the numbers falling?

ROSSI: Well, some of the numbers on the high side are just simply lies. They are made up numbers. You could call them guesstimates made to startle and amaze. I get frequent telephone calls from the press, asking, "How many homeless do you think there are, Professor Rossi?" And I will say, "Oh, six hundred thousand." And they just hang up. They don't want to use that number. If I had said, "Two or three million," they would have used it. But six hundred thousand, no. Incidentally, that is the number I think is actually closest to the case.

GRUNBERG: Perhaps it is six hundred thousand from a pool of three million extremely poor persons.

ROSSI: Right, I would say that the pool of precariously housed, extremely poor persons numbers around three million.

GIAMO: Speaking about the incidence of poverty and homelessness today reminds me of those voices that have come before us. For example, in 1933 George Orwell published his classic first-person account of poverty, *Down and Out in Paris and London*. And now, sixty years later, you've come out with a book, *Down and Out in America*. I'm wondering what the two titles suggest about the history of destitution. Your choice of title seems to indicate a continuity.

ROSSI: Continuity is hard to say but, certainly, there have always been people who were on the bottom and defined as outside of society—who didn't really have any connections with kin or with institutions, nor did the institutions take any responsibility for them. And that was the case in the old Bowery for the unattached old persons. The responsibility for them has now been taken up by the social security system, if you qualify, and most people do. But nowadays young extremely poor unattached males and females are tossed out of their kinship networks and society does not want to take any responsibility for them.

GRUNBERG: That reminds me of something you wrote about in your book. You discussed the fact that there used to be two concepts of homelessness, a particular town's local homeless and its outsider homeless.

ROSSI: That's right. That was because of the settlement rules that used to govern who was eligible for local public welfare. The settlement rules were tossed out by the Supreme Court in 1964. You see, in order for a person to become eligible for any kind of welfare relief he or she had to have been a resident of the locality in question. This goes back to colonial times and the Elizabethan poor laws, which stated that each parish had to take care of its own poor, the maimed and the sick, and the like. So the question always arose: well, who is "ours"? So, for example, in New York state during the depression, the settlement rule required that you be a resident of the state for at least a year, and of the county for at least six months, in order to become eligible for poor relief. Because one consequence of the depression was a great deal of transiency, a distinction then had to be made between "our homeless" and the "transient homeless" just passing through. The transients were just pushed along with Greyhound therapy to the next town or county.

GRUNBERG: Which worked a little bit when there were jobs.

ROSSI: Not in the depression years. There were no jobs. There were huge transient camps. I remember one in Buffalo that I read about because it was the subject of social research. There was a study run by a psychologist who got the job of being the research director of a transient camp in Buffalo. I think there was something like twenty thousand people going through that camp in the course of about six months. The research he undertook and later published [Herman J. P. Schubert, *Twenty Thousand Transients: A Year's Sample of Those Who Apply for Aid in a Northern City* (1935)] was undertaken by white-collar transients whom he put to work making handtabs of each person who came in with such information as age, sex, etc. The transients were largely young men who went from place to place looking for work.

GRUNBERG: Why didn't all the homeless go back to their localities and demand help?

ROSSI: Well, this was during the depression and the transient homeless were on the lookout for jobs. There was nothing available in their own hometowns. These young men, 18–22 years old, would hook a ride to Buffalo, or Cleveland, or wherever. They'd land there, find nothing, move on, and, pretty soon, having lost the settlement rights in their own hometowns, they would only stay for a little while before, being pushed out by their struggling families, they would move on again.

GRUNBERG: So this movement was more job oriented? There was no welfare system?

ROSSI: There has never been a welfare system for unattached men. You have to be attached.

GIAMO: One gets the picture that this dislocation has been traditionally associated with men, whereas today a lot more people are becoming outsiders to society, women and children, for example.

ROSSI: Well, women and children are not that far outside. The Aid to Families with Dependent Children [AFDC] system will take care of them at least to some degree, niggardly, but at least to some degree. But the so-called able-bodied, unattached male of working age is the person who is really the most uncared for. You might call it the masculinization of poverty. Well, the poverty of single persons has always been masculinized.

GIAMO: What do you think has changed about homelessness and what do you think has remained constant over the years?

ROSSI: I think that what has remained constant is that these are people who are outsiders in a society which is really organized around family units. What is different is that, at least, there used to be a need for people in the economy who could move from place to place, or follow the crops, or be on tap for major construction jobs. Transient people were important to the economy. In fact, there are many who would say that the Bowery—and homelessness and transiency—was necessary for society. There were jobs that had to be done and could only be done by people who could pick up and move from place to place at a moment's notice. So transiency was a part of capitalism. Now there is no productive niche for these people in our society or, rather, we are unable to come up with what the niche is or should be.

GIAMO: Do you think that the problem of homelessness over the past 100 years reflects the nature of society as a whole? It seems as though the homeless outsider in America has journeyed from the freight train to the shelter. Historically, the hobo, often a romanticized figure of the waning frontier, represented the migratory working life in an age of industrial expansion. Hobohemia, or skid row, represented the segregated, stationary life in an age of industrial surplus when the migration to urban financial centers was fast being realized. The "bum" was a hobo who had reached the end of the line—who was indeed down-and-out, yet, as you say, managed to work sporadically as an "odd-jobber" and supply some needed demand for the casual labor market. What story does contemporary homelessness reveal about our present state?

ROSSI: What does it say about today's society? I think that we are in a transition where the economy is really becoming a world economy. We are also a much more humane society than we were in the past. We worry about these people. We don't do what we did in the 1930s when the cops just threw these people in jail, or herded them into the appropriate spots, or loaded them on the train. So we treat them more gently.

GRUNBERG: What message do we want to send to the homeless? Should we let them know that gentleness awaits them?

ROSSI: As a military policeman during World War II, I learned that you never order people to do something they cannot do. So you don't say I am not going to feed you anymore until you get a job. That would be harsh and unreasonable because there are few, if any, employment opportunities for the homeless young men.

GRUNBERG: The old adage, teach them to fish.

ROSSI: Right, just show me the river. Give me a pole and show me a river.

GRUNBERG: What of those few who say they do not wish to work right now?

ROSSI: Well, I am not someone who wishes to see anyone starve. So you might have to put those people into some sort of structured environment or institution. There are degrees of deterioration beyond which you do have to warehouse people.

GIAMO: Who are the people we are talking about today?

ROSSI: The most optimistic prospects among all of the homeless people today are the homeless families—the females with their children. That may be almost entirely fixable by raising the welfare benefits and helping them a little. Then you have persons who are at the end of the trail of going constantly downhill: petty crime, prison sentences, alcoholism, drug abuse, etc. By the time they get to the Keener Building or the Fort Washington Armory [New York City shelters] they are pretty far deteriorated. I do not know how you get them out of that. These are the guys who are 32 years old, but look 45. You see this too in the maximum security prison system. You go up and ask them what they will do when they get out and they say, "I will go home to my mother for a little while and then I will probably come back here."

GRUNBERG: "Don't worry, I'll be back."

ROSSI: That's right. "It's nice here. I know how to handle this world." Anyway, the unattached male is the largest problem. Is there some sort of job which could be provided so that he could become reattached to the world? I am not sure.

GIAMO: To what extent do you think race is a factor?

ROSSI: It is race which makes them vulnerable to being plucked out of the economy. Race and poor education, etc.

GRUNBERG: Often these facts are used to fuel racist commentary. "The Irish never faced these problems, and the Jews got out of the ghettos."

ROSSI: Well, we have lost perspective then, because in the nineteenth century the problems of the Irish were exactly what the problems of the blacks are today. A lot of female-headed households, a lot of homeless young men who were transients. The Bowery was full of Irish and Germans, but they got out of it because the economy changed. The old men on the Bowery did not get out of the Bowery because social security went up and they could afford better lives. They died off. The young Irish tramps, they died off too. But it was their successors who did not get in there. It is like whole generations got thrown away.

GIAMO: In 1985, 40 percent of black males under the age of 35 were unemployed.

ROSSI: Well I think that we are seeing the end result of that 40 percent back then. It is part of the isolation of the black community from the rest of society. If you [Giamo] need a job, there is someone you know who can tell you where a job is. If your friends and family are also persons who do not know of any jobs—and they might be looking as well—then you are out of the network of referrals.

I have forgotten now who did this, but one's range of knowledge and acquaintance in the world makes a difference. Researchers asked people certain questions like "Do you know a doctor?" "Do you know someone who owns a factory?" "Or who owns a business?" "Or who works in the post office?" They found that blacks have a very restricted range of acquaintances.

GRUNBERG: Access?

ROSSI: Information access.

GIAMO: Other racial and ethnic minorities are also over represented among today's homeless.

ROSSI: That's right, Hispanics, and the American Indian probably is the worst in this regard. The homeless in Minneapolis are something like 20 to 25 percent American Indian.

GIAMO: We've talked about race, gender, and ethnicity as being parts of the overall homeless picture, economics as well, but what about culture?

ROSSI: I am sure it does fit in, I just don't know how to conceptualize it. Certainly part of any person's culture is the extent to which one holds obligation to kin. So, now, probably the most familistic of our American ethnic groups are the Irish. The most familistic are the ones who can afford it. So the Irish are in the position where they have a very strong sense of obligation to siblings, to nephews, nieces, parents, grandparents, children, grandchildren, and the like; and they can afford it. They are now in a very affluent position.

Blacks have an interesting kind of kinship set of obligations. (I am talking here of research my wife and I have done for the last four or five years, recently published as *Of Human Bonding*.) It is much flatter. Blacks feel a flatter level of obligation to a wider network of kin. That is the basis of the black network Carol Stack researched where people can very easily develop a kinship sense of obligation in relationships with first, second, and third cousins. In a circumstance where there is some affluence in there, it would be a fantastic way of getting along. It would be like the Koreans who help each other and make fictitious kin, and the like. But, without affluence, it can be like a maintenance network, rather than a growth network.

GRUNBERG: Is the profile of Chicago's homeless similar to other cities?

ROSSI: Yes, with the exception of the racial composition, which may vary from place to place. Actually, ratios of races and ethnic groups vary mysteriously in one sense. In Detroit, Chicago, and New York, blacks dominate the homeless picture. But in Birmingham, Alabama? No, it's whites. Now what makes for these differences? I do not know. Maybe there is subtle discrimination in the shelter systems. Where do the black homeless go in Birmingham?

GRUNBERG: Apparently where white researchers don't go.

ROSSI: Apparently. Actually, a researcher, Leonard Blumberg, who studied the homeless in the 1950s in Philadelphia found very few blacks on that city's skid row. He raised the question "Where are the black homeless?" And he speculated that they must have been taken care of inside the black ghetto. You see, he hadn't gone into the black ghetto of Philadelphia to see how the extremely poor were taken care of there. So maybe the case is that in Birmingham, somehow or another, the blacks take care of their dependent adults in that environment more so than they do in New York. Or maybe there is a black skid row as well as a white one.

GIAMO: But that really parallels a lot of people's observation about the black migration to the North after World War II, which helped to uproot some of that group and perhaps set the stage for what we are now seeing—homelessness among the second- and third-generation black ghetto residents.

ROSSI: It would be interesting to look at the white Appalachian migrants who came to Detroit, Cleveland, and Pittsburgh, also after World War II. They were the people who fueled the rise of what is now the Rustbelt industry. What happened to these migrants who came North after World War II?

GIAMO: I remember a Cleveland section. It was called "hillbilly haven"; it was on the west side of town and the black ghetto was on the east side.

ROSSI: Those people lived in their cars in the following sense. They would come up to Cleveland, get jobs, get fired, and go back to West Virginia for a while, and then come back. There was a sense of some community they could go back to, a home "where they have to let you in" in that hollow back there. They were expected to go back and forth.

The blacks could not go back to the South. They stayed. They could not go back, just like William Kennedy's hero in *Ironweed*. Well, there is another difference. The hillbillies return when they fail.

GIAMO: What we talk about when we talk about homelessness is often the result of our approach to the social problem. In your opinion, how has methodology evolved over the years, say from the early Chicago School of sociology to your present demographic approach?

ROSSI: Well, part of the old Chicago School—Robert Park, etc.—was what I call "gee whiz" sociology. It is the kind of thing which appears in *Parade* magazine or the *New York Times* magazine. "Gee whiz," there are those terrible people, or these sad people. But the aim is to startle and amaze and to attract attention. So you look at exotic populations, the Gold Coast and the slum, or the Jewish ghetto, street corner society, and the like. You look at them and you stare and you say, "Hey, they're different from us and everybody ought to know about them because they *are* different."

Now we are saying that homelessness is a recognized social problem. We see people out there on the street. We can go in there and say, like Kim Hopper, "Wow, look at these interesting cases that you should be aware of because then you would be more sympathetic if you knew more about them. For example, this poor woman of 45 years who lives out of a shopping bag and who was thrown out of her home by her sister." And so on. Kim Hopper's work is in this "gee whiz" tradition.

My perspective is that, yes, there probably are people like those Kim Hopper wishes to point out, but we have to know what the central tendencies are in this population so that we do not just look at the sympathetic types or the unusual types or the exotic types.

G R U N B E R G: We want to avoid setting policy based on the exception.

R O S S I: Exactly. You do not want to set policy based on exceptions. You want to get the big picture, which is a dull tale made up of headcounts, averages, and standard deviations accumulated over long periods of time, indicating where in our society there are large groups of people who are getting the dirty end of the stick.

G R U N B E R G: When I get the opportunity to speak to people about homelessness, I often say that nowadays there seem to be fewer people who have descended into homelessness from significantly higher levels. It seems that people are more likely to have been "born" into homelessness. By the time they are 25 years old, they have led lives which have pointed them toward the shelter system. In this sense, they are suffering not so much from lack of a "home," but from a homeless lifestyle.

R O S S I: They are losing continuously.

G R U N B E R G: Yes. Yet people have this notion that today's homeless were all doing very well and fell great distances down into homelessness.

R O S S I: It is a ridiculous position.

G R U N B E R G: Do you think that this is, in part, a result of the coalition advocacy type of perspective?

R O S S I: Yes, and it is also a theme of the advocates that "there, but for the grace of God, go I." That we are all just one paycheck away from homelessness.

GRUNBERG: This gets us back to an essential point. We touched on it a bit earlier when we made reference to the rhetoric of homelessness. If, for example, you refer to *the* social problem as homelessness, then it is clear—a "home" will solve the problem. So should we be calling it something else? For instance, the late Michael Harrington referred to the homeless as the "uprooted."

GIAMO: That's right. He felt that the notion of "uprootedness" would connect the social problem to the root systems of capitalism, from preindustrial to industrial and postindustrial forms.

ROSSI: That's what was meant by "homelessness" in the 1930s. What they really meant were people who did not have any families.

GRUNBERG: You mean the construct of "disaffiliation" as the sociologists Howard Bahr, Donald Bogue, Theodore Caplow, and others presented it.

ROSSI: Yes. Disaffiliation referred to the old men who were thrown out by their families or the families just did not want anything to do with them for behavioral reasons, or whatever. They were sort of the born losers, who maybe had marginal jobs and were perfectly okay for the first twenty years or so. But then the kids grew up and they said, "Let's get the old bastard out of here." And they pushed him out.

Now what is going on with the homeless today is that the mothers are saying, "Okay, you have been a 'bum' for the last five or six years and you're not getting anywhere; you're a big burden. I need the room for the other kids—get out."

GIAMO: In the early part of your book, you mentioned that the more you looked into homelessness, the more it seemed to be misstated.

ROSSI: It has been misstated as a housing problem. I think it is really quite unfortunate that the term "homeless" became transferred to this uprooted population. I kind of like Harrington's term because the notion of roots also conveys connectedness to an environment that sustains you.

GIAMO: As he put it: "A 'home' is not simply a roof over one's head. It is the center of a web of human relationships. When the web is shredded as a result of social and economic trends, a person is homeless even if he or she has an anonymous room somewhere" [*The New American Poverty* (1984)].

GRUNBERG: That is why I call the approach I take to working with single homeless men "social networking." In fact, one of the best operating mottos that these homeless relate very well to is that "a man has got to have people behind him." They hear it and they take to it and, all throughout the time I am working with them, they often bring it back to me.

ROSSI: That is very interesting. Let me tell you about an interesting book that I picked up recently, called *Street Woman*, by Eleanor Miller, an assistant professor who talked to women who were in a halfway house. What she did was try to reconcile Carol Stack's notion of the network of supporting people that blacks who were very, very poor— women, in particular—had developed. It was a network of reciprocal care and habits, and she says: "What has happened to these people [in the halfway house]; didn't they have that?" And they don't, and the reason they don't is that they cannot reciprocate. Those loose, extended kin or pseudo-kin networks were sustained by each individual being able to contribute something. But these people cannot reciprocate, and this is hostile to the development of a network.

Based upon this whole notion of uprootedness, I've moved into looking at the extremely poor who are *not* unconnected, who are housed, and who are managing to get along. I did a little bit of that with the General Assistance clients as well as those clients receiving AFDC in Chicago. There is a very large number of unattached adults sustained mostly by their parents. These are people who are between 25 and 55 years old with essentially zero income. They are living with their parents. Perhaps you could think of your own families and see where a cousin, or a friend of someone you know who has returned home jobless or has gone several months with no income, might be in the same boat. Maybe someone who is a borderline mental defective, or maybe someone who has a chronic mental illness. I think that, literally, there are millions of people living like that, living off and on with their families, maybe for half a year, then they are out for a bit on their own. They lose a job and they come back. They are precariously on the edge of being in shelters.

My guess is that they are somewhat acceptable in their behavior. They can reciprocate. They are not floridly psychotic, or criminal, or too aggressive. They are the ordinary American "schlump." They may go on a drinking or drug binge and, when they do, they don't come home. Otherwise, they're back and forth. I haven't been able to make a precise estimate, but it is my guess that something in the order of two to three million people live like this.

GRUNBERG: Is this the number that advocacy groups are counting? Does this account for the discrepancy in numbers?

ROSSI: God knows. The coalition does not really like to talk about these people. They prefer to talk about families. I mean, these are not terribly sympathetic types, quite unlike the notion of this guy who was working at one point for General Motors in a Flint, Michigan, plant, and then one day Roger Smith just up and throws him out. You know the rest of the story. The laid-off worker takes a job at McDonald's and that closed down, so he works at a car wash and lives in a trailer for a while. Then he has to sell the trailer, and so on. Well, that is not one of these guys. The people I'm referring to have never really had anything. They are only marginally able to support themselves for periods of time.

This is largely reconstruction because I do not yet have longitudinal data that will show it, but I will have the data in several months or so.

GIAMO: In your book, you defined literal homelessness as not having customary access to a conventional dwelling, but, as you reveal, people who are precariously housed or connected are at risk of becoming homeless.

ROSSI: The one-fifth of the precariously housed who become homeless fluctuates in terms of what our economy is doing. This is why we saw our skid row populations decline from 1950 to 1980 as social security took a lot of the old men out of the group. So I think if we had full employment, say within the space of ten years, the pool of extremely poor would decline, as would the proportion of persons who are literally homeless, until what you were left over with would be the disabled.

GRUNBERG: So there is movement between the extremely poor and the homeless, but is there much movement between the extremely poor and the poor, and between the poor and the working class, and so on?

ROSSI: Between the extremely poor and the poor there is a lot of movement. The Current Population Survey of 1988 shows that 20 percent of the extremely poor in 1987 were no longer extremely poor in 1988. Evidently they lost their jobs, they had some setbacks, got divorced, and went to live with their parents. Then they reassembled themselves in 1988 and went back on their own, back into the ranks of the poor. There is the same amount of movement the other way, for the same reasons.

GIAMO: Your research has shown a 224 percent increase in extreme poverty since 1973. What made for such a dramatic rise?

ROSSI: The dislocation of the economy where all those manufacturing jobs for unskilled and semiskilled workers disappeared. It really started around 1975.

GRUNBERG: And $4,000 is the level below which you consider someone extremely poor?

ROSSI: I've changed that slightly. My level is one-half that of the poverty line. I think that for a single person now it is $3,000. For larger families, it is adjusted depending on how many kids there are; but it doesn't go over $6,000.

GRUNBERG: For a single person, that is around $55–$60 income each week.

ROSSI: One way of looking at the whole social problem is this: how can we construct, or reconstruct, the resources and abilities of the families to take care of their failures? I had this odd program which I was told to include in my book, and I did. It is called Aid to Families with Dependent Adults [AFDA]. This program would provide subsidies, especially to poor families, so that they are able to sustain whatever additional expenses are necessary to keep their dependent adults inside the house. Supplemental Security Income does that, though it is indirect. An SSI payment will get your mother to take you back, providing you share a bit of it with her.

GRUNBERG: For many of the homeless, the only form of connectedness with their families is through the vehicle of their checks. Their checks allow them to go home. An individual, for instance, can buy someone dinner or offer some sort of gift. For those few days, a person can experience a sort of status that eludes him or her ordinarily. I think you're onto something with your AFDA program, mainly because income allows for a certain type of reciprocity. Perhaps this would lead to other reciprocal acts.

ROSSI: You would have to worry about who would qualify and, also, you would have to make sure the family got their share.

This might sound like a bypass, but it is really quite relevant. The Edna McConnell Clark Foundation in New York has been funding programs throughout the country for what it calls family preservation. It is aimed at young adolescents who are about ready to be removed from their families because of conflict with the family, unruly adults, child abuse, etc. The members of the foundation have this notion that there is enough residual, positive affect in families so that they can do something for the family in a very short period of time. It is very intensive work with the family—about four weeks in length and workers are on call 24 hours a day. They can prevent the child from being removed from the home and stabilize the circumstances so that neither the child gets hurt nor the family suffers too much. They attempt to work out accommodative behavior. We need some program like this for unattached adults who are about to be thrown out of their families.

GIAMO: Those people who fall out from the extremely poor and land amid the ranks of the homeless are more vulnerable than those who have remained precariously attached. What sorts of "disabilities" are involved that separate the homeless from the extremely poor? I believe you discussed about half a dozen, including unemployment, social isolation, and crime.

ROSSI: And mental illness, poor physical health, and long-term alcohol and drug abuse. Persons with one or more of these disabilities can be considered most vulnerable. They are more vulnerable because the labor market opportunities are slimmer due to these disabilities.

GRUNBERG: So disabilities should be seen in terms of access to employment? They are seen functionally.

ROSSI: Exactly. And these are the same disabilities which make it difficult for them to maintain relationships and networks. That creates social isolation.

GRUNBERG: If you have a criminal record in your past, you are disabled because it is preventing employment. But aren't people going to say, "Why should he be given a job? He burglarized three stores."

ROSSI: That is why he should be considered functionally disabled—because no one will hire him.

GRUNBERG: Should anyone hire him?

ROSSI: Sure. He should not be put in charge of the cash register, but he should be given something to do.

GIAMO: When you broaden the definition of disability to include unemployment and crime, you cover the whole range of factors that create and perpetuate homelessness.

GRUNBERG: And you tie it all together economically.

ROSSI: There will always be people who cannot get it together due to disabilities and you can only warehouse them. Of course, the warehouses should be safe and humane.

GIAMO: Do you think that it is possible to eliminate poverty?

ROSSI: Sure. It is all relative. Even the homeless in our shelters are better off than the homeless on the streets of Calcutta. If we had full employment and we doubled the average personal income in the United States, we would just have persons who would be homeless, but living at a higher level of life.

GIAMO: But if you are poor, your frame of reference is based on the society you are living in. So no matter where you are, if you are at the bottom, aren't you experiencing the same misery as some outcast would feel, say, in Bangladesh?

ROSSI: There is no doubt of that but, from the point of view of the physical, our homeless are not as emaciated or wasted as the homeless in Bangladesh. Their health is better and their access to health care is better.

GRUNBERG: Even if they remain demoralized?

ROSSI: I doubt whether or not you would see obese people among the beggars of Calcutta, but you will see them among the homeless here.

GIAMO: You have observed, though, that homeless people today are suffering from multiple disabilities.

ROSSI: The majority have at least one, and the overlap between various disabilities is quite high.

GIAMO: Do you think that our social service system is geared toward dealing with multiple disabilities in the same person?

ROSSI: Hell no. Our mental health system doesn't like to deal with alcoholics, and so on. I would worry about that if I thought the mental health industry knew what to do about mental illness, but they don't; or if the alcoholism industry knew what to do about alcoholism.

GIAMO: You have written that you view the chronic homeless as "victims of perverse macrolevel social forces" [*Down and Out in America* (1989)].

R o s s i: Right, compounded by their vulnerability. The persons we have to focus upon are the extremely poor. We have to diminish the size of that pool so that there will not be so many who are so vulnerable, pushed over the brink, and catapulted into homelessness.

G i a m o: You seem to place the blame on major institutions: the housing market, the labor market, and the social welfare system. How is each of these institutions responsible?

R o s s i: I think that the labor market is probably the biggest engine in that trio. The loss of unskilled jobs is the base of it. The housing market comes out of our mistaken notion that we should get rid of those hotels, those skid row places. So we lost the capacity to house most unattached persons who can only afford a dollar or two for rent each night. It is also the case that nobody can build housing which can compete with the shelters. If we got rid of the shelters, maybe the housing market would respond in kind.

The welfare system is implicated in the following way: we do not have a substantial safety net for unattached, able-bodied men. Historically, we did have one before inflation lowered its value. It is what supported the old men on skid rows. If you are well-connected and you have a chronic mental illness, you can get SSI. Being well-connected means you have somebody who can get you through that maze, who is intelligent enough to manipulate that bureaucracy. A case-worker could do it. If you are not well-connected, if you are like that famous homeless woman in New York City—"Billie Boggs"—you are not going to get yourself through that system.

There is a former graduate student of mine who has been on SSI for thirty years and he never gets bounced off. He says he is not crazy. In fact, he says, "I'd be crazy if I didn't collect SSI." Okay, so we need a welfare system that is not designed to keep people off but to cover people who need it. We could get rid of homeless females and their kids very easily by changing the AFDC system so that it provides enough money to actually rent a house.

GIAMO: About 60 percent of Reagan's budget cuts of the early eighties were directed at programs that were helping the poor. Do you see that as another "macrolevel" process which can be pointed to?

ROSSI: Actually, most of the damage was done before Reagan came into office. The inflationary surge from 1974 to 1980 wiped out the AFDC. In fact, Reagan's housing policy was not bad. He didn't authorize very much in the way of public housing construction, but the provision of housing vouchers has meant that literally millions of people have been and are being helped in their housing. The HUD voucher system is a very good way to help.

GRUNBERG: Well, it is money that is targeted and cannot be used in any other way. Someone ought to do a study of how society would actually save money by doing these sorts of things. While a barracks-like shelter for single men and women may only cost $30–$40 per person per day, the longer you stay in one, the longer you will probably need costlier, long-term interventions. Less money would be wasted in the long run if it could be appropriately spent at the outset.

ROSSI: I have always had the notion that programs such as the one I suggested in my book—Aid to Families with Dependent Adults—would actually save money. If you could help a family keep their dependent adult, it would probably cost around $6,000 per year. That is cheap. Taking somebody in for a short-term stay in a mental hospital costs around $2,000 or more each month. AFDA would be cheaper.

GRUNBERG: Let me ask you this. Twenty years from now, what is it all going to look like?

ROSSI: The economy, by some difficult process, will work out a place for these young black or Hispanic men. We are now in a period of transition, where there have been rapid changes in our economy and, therefore, in our labor force which we have not fully adjusted to. This transition took place between 1974 (with that oil crisis) and 1985. There is a whole generation of young men and women too—the female-headed households, who were left out of the transition—who were stuck in this ghastly business.

The reason which makes me think that this is an important source of today's homeless problems on a macrolevel is that it is occurring in England, France, Italy, and the like, and in the same age, sex, and marital status groups.

GIAMO: This is a global problem affecting most industrialized nation-states.

ROSSI: Absolutely. I would not be surprised to see this occur in Moscow.

GRUNBERG: Germany is already experiencing this.

ROSSI: The Germans, as well as the Swedes, have an interesting way of handling these problems. The lower level of their occupational structure is occupied by "guest workers." So what these countries will do is ship the Turks back to Turkey, the Yugoslavs back to Yugoslavia, the southern Italians back to Sicily, etc.

GIAMO: And while these "guest workers" were in their respective host countries, they were given jobs and housing.

ROSSI: Right. There were jobs for them but, once they are surplus, they are shipped out.

This has become one world in a very literal sense. The prosperity of the Republic of Korea, for example, is bought partially at the expense of our marginal people who have now become homeless. Therefore, we have to think of ways in which we can connect people with jobs they can do. And we have to work to prevent the deterioration of the everyday life they experience in their adolescence. By the time they become literally homeless out on the street, and their families do not want them, there is a great deal of deterioration.

A friend of mine is running a research program on the underclass. I said to him, "The homeless belong in there," and he said, in effect, "Let's forget about it; there's nothing you can do about them. It's too late. Let's triage on this, let's support them somehow, set up warehouses, or whatever."

GRUNBERG: Fifty-bed or twenty-bed warehouses, with some support, etc.

ROSSI: Right, nice warehouses. But we have to avoid this. We have to do something early on. We can provide a set of jobs that people can do, that provides a minimal kind of economic level, that helps them to reciprocate. Additionally, we have to provide incentives for people to support each other, to get married, to keep their kids with them, and so on.

GIAMO: What are your short- and long-term recommendations for addressing the problems of homelessness?

ROSSI: The short-term recommendation is that we have to supply shelter and food for people's needs. The long-term recommendations are that, first of all, we have got to stop the irresponsible deinstitutionalization of people. So we have to warehouse the chronically mentally ill. We need to revive the YMCA and the other inexpensive hotels too. Also, we have to provide employment opportunities for young people, men and women. Even if that would require setting up public employment devices. I can't believe that we don't need to replace the streets of New York, clean up Tompkins Square Park, fill the potholes, etc. Those are the things that the Works Progress Administration [WPA], the Civil Works Administration [CWA], and the Civilian Conservation Corps [CCC] used to do. Anything we do of this sort would also provide plenty of employment for middle-class people in the areas of management and training. This was also one of the functions of the WPA and the CWA. They provided employment at a variety of levels. There may have been cheaper ways you could have built the main terminal at La Guardia airport (other than have the WPA build it), but it was a socially useful method.

GRUNBERG: In your opinion, should it be a constitutional right for every citizen to have a home and a job?

ROSSI: Yes. That would be nice. There should be a constitutional right for every person to have an opportunity for a job. Right now the current legislation under our constitution provides for equal opportunity, but not that there must be an opportunity for everybody. If there are a thousand job applications for one job, maybe everybody has an equal chance for that job, but only one person is going to get a job. If there are a thousand applications, there should be a thousand jobs.

JERZY KOSINSKI

Chance Beings

BENEDICT GIAMO: Since so much of a society's approach to homelessness depends upon the eye through which it sees the problem, I was hoping that you could elaborate on your own particular perspective that you bring to the social situation. Consider this a preface to the interview.

JERZY KOSINSKI: Well, then, let me first qualify the optics, the lenses that I will use to view homelessness. One lens is going to be very wide angle and that stems from my background in Eastern Europe, being uprooted together with everybody else in 1939. Homelessness is, therefore, a state imposed from outside when societies are in a state of war. War, of course, is homelessness. It presupposes destruction, the breaking up of the family. One could say that a state of war is a state of homelessness. A soldier is homeless. At best, war is a temporary shelter.

Homelessness also means less-than-home. It presupposes somehow that one ought to have a home and that, therefore, a homeless person is somehow deprived of something that some other people may take for granted. Here I'm referring to the second aspect of the wide-angle lens, the collective state where homes belong to the state, which means you are already less-than-home. Now, if you ask me, "Do you own this home?" I would say, "No, I rent. Why do I rent? I don't want to own. I want to be, to a degree, homeless." Let me further narrow this point of view. Consider being homeless in a country in which having a home is taken as a status. In fact, it is something one works toward as a kind of tenure (comparable to the tenure system in academia). Well, to someone from Eastern Europe who was uprooted and who could have faced destruction, not having a home is a rather minor dramatic predicament in life. I would take it far more for granted that I could be expelled from my domain tomorrow morning by forces other than the landlord's. Perhaps my American counterpart would say, "What? What do you mean they treat you like this? What right do they have?" And I would say, "Well, you know they could have killed me." We have to start with that premise.

I should add that I came from a Communist state that fraudulently assured a shelter, while taking away the notion of self. The state provided minimum services for the body, while taking maximum means away from the mind. In fact, it very openly conducted this transaction by saying, "I'm giving you a home. I'm giving your kid a breakfast and a luncheon and a resemblance of dinner; and I'm giving you education and medical services. True, I'm taking care of your physical being. However, I parenthetically add that there will be nothing parenthetical about this condition. There will be no parenthesis in which you will be able to conduct your own affairs in any way you want. You will be mercifully treated, but at the mercy that can be merciless." Now that condition is given.

Narrowing further to the more or less average point of view, or the regular sociological lens, leads to a focus on two subjects: the nineteenth century in Europe, which was the century of the homeless (where the middle class was just developing and all the various Marxist parties came into being), and the American family. These were my two specialties. In a way, these two broad areas summarize a basic dialectic of the nineteenth century: establishing the middle-class ethos or destroying it. The former can be seen in American society, which has the most predictable middle-class fortress, and where the notion of "home" is essential; the latter can be evidenced in the Communist movement that emerged during this time in European societies.

Therefore, narrowing it even further, I look at the homeless not from the society's point of view, but from the point of view of the homeless person himself or herself. And I can tell you exactly what my focus is and about my concern, my preoccupation. Right now I'm looking at a specific design of a home on wheels. It's a cart that you see in this neighborhood. Actually, it's a version of a cart; call it a "vehicle" if you want to be very American about it. It's a four-wheel vehicle, a sort of shopping cart, that most of the homeless in this neighborhood would steal to have. The concept I'm working on is just this type of shopping cart that would collapse into a portable home in which one can carry one's belongings, open it at night, lock oneself in it, take the wheels off, put the wheels inside, close oneself off from the outside—and be safe from heat, from frost (far more importantly), and from being hit over the head when asleep by someone else in the neighborhood. Not even a police club can break it. There is also a window made of fiberglass.

GIAMO: You even put a picture window into that device.

KOSINSKI: Yes, indeed, so you can see who else is out there. You can look at other people's homes.

G I A M O : Which is a major middle-class preoccupation as well.

K O S I N S K I : This is basically the concept of home that I'm working on for the homeless. Call it a mini-van home.

J E F F R E Y   G R U N B E R G : No motor, it's all push?

K O S I N S K I : It's self-propelled—Self with a capital *S*—since in this case I have great respect for the homeless individual, whom I refuse to see as a victim of society and I refuse to see as a victim of his or her own self. I see the homeless person as a chance being at the mercy of forces that he or she was not able to figure out or may not be able to figure out. And if he or she cannot figure out the state of homelessness, why should he or she when the state cannot figure it out either?

Narrowing it further, if this community (one of the most affluent neighborhoods of New York City) isn't smart enough to resolve the fact that there are people who have no place to sleep, why should the homeless be smart enough to resolve their own predicaments? Are the avenues to "home" as simple as that? Clearly they are not.

G R U N B E R G : Is the community not smart enough or is there something intentional about its desire to watch some people suffer? Is racism a part of the social problem?

K O S I N S K I : I prefer to see it (I say "prefer" because maybe it is a way of wishful thinking or of wishful seeing) as a community not being smart enough, not being intelligent enough, pragmatic enough to realize the dimensions of the problem. The homeless have very little to lose and very little vested interest in the notion of order, home, and the philosophy of having in a society which is based on free enterprise. So I'd like to think that a society that allows the state of homelessness to continue (providing that the homeless person wants to have a home) is a society not smart enough to resolve the problem.

G I A M O : What does homelessness reveal then about American society? Or let's say the American dream?

KOSINSKI: Homeless people in my neighborhoods, whether in New Haven, where there are a great number of homeless people right outside the fortress of Yale, or here in New York, cause one to establish a new parameter. One should accept that these are a category of people who cannot afford a standard mobile home, since there is right above them a category of people who can. Homelessness then, according to this view, is a perfectly valid category of the free enterprise system. For whatever reason, this person who is homeless finds himself or herself in a mini-enterprise. This mini-enterprise is reduced to asking for help, for money, from passersby. Now had this homeless person been a foundation, this would have been considered a tax-deductible operation. If one were to make this condition tax-deductible, as with the Jewish Presence Foundation of which I am president, then this person—and the needs of this person—would and should be tax-deductible. Hence the mini-van home would serve such a purpose.

GRUNBERG: You're going to upset a lot of people if your idea takes off.

KOSINSKI: I don't know whether the mini-van home should upset people or the sight of someone who is frostbitten in the morning.

GRUNBERG: Which would bother people more?

KOSINSKI: Simply put, it is just a condition that is very prevalent to-day on the streets. It is a condition to be acknowledged, regardless of whether it is bothersome or not. It is certainly bothersome to the person who is frostbitten. It can also be bothersome to some individuals who pass this person by, and to assume that everyone is indifferent to someone else's misery may simply not be true. It could be safely assumed that people with homes, which in the winter are very warm, can take far less enjoyment from their well-deserved homes by seeing a homeless person sleeping at the entrance to their homes. Hence the myth of the pursuit of happiness—or the reality of it—can be infringed upon by the sight of someone who simply doesn't participate as fully in this society.

GRUNBERG: We can rest comfortably knowing that the homeless are not freezing?

KOSINSKI: Precisely. This means that some sleeplessness of my own could be reduced by the fact that the homeless are no longer frostbitten, but sleep in mini-van homes of their own which protect them from frost, attacks by dogs, drunkards, and drug addicts—or attacks by those who simply want to experience the power of their own hands or feet on someone else's flesh.

Therefore, I don't want to enter into an argument with myself or with anyone else relative to what is right or what is wrong. I'm too pragmatic for that and too philosophical. What interests me is the degree to which one can accept the state of homelessness as being a given, an inherited given perhaps, and as being unavoidable (I haven't seen it resolved, at least not in American society). And I have not been able to convince those who are in charge of wealth that they should help those who can no longer help themselves, because the notion that people should be able to help themselves is a very firm Protestant notion. You see, the first project which I embarked on in the mid-1960s involved coming up with some 400 people who were absolutely unable—not unwilling but unable—to help themselves because they were addicted to wine; they were heavy drinkers of American wine.

GIAMO: Down on the Bowery?

KOSINSKI: Yes, the Bowery. And I tried to talk to friends of mine who would routinely donate very expensive pieces of furniture to various American museums, including the Museum of Modern Art and, in particular, the Metropolitan Museum of Art. I tried to tell them that one commode of Louis XIV, given to a tax-deductible project that could be formed for the Bowery homeless, would prove to be a truly priceless investment. The money would have been used for those who could no longer help themselves, an open project to be called "the I can no longer help myself project." As a homeless person, I therefore have to be maintained by society and should be treated no differently than those on welfare. Remember, welfare presupposes treating "well" those who no longer "fare well" by themselves. Well, I failed miserably, even with the most immediate members of my own family at the time. My late wife felt that this was not an attitude to be encouraged and that, however useful the help extended to the few hundred individuals might be, the example it would set would be derogatory—that it would, in fact, diminish the whole ethos of work and the philosophy of achievement that is to be propagated. Therefore, it would make sense to give the same money, or possibly more, to the foundation devoted to the very opposite—helping those who can help themselves.

GRUNBERG: How did you respond to that?

KOSINSKI: I accept someone else's view the way I accept my own. We are in a country of free expression.

GIAMO: It reminds me of a part of your novel *The Devil Tree*, in which the protagonist, Jonathan Whalen, proposes such a Bowery project to the wife of his business partner, a wealthy financier. Of course, she shoots it down.

KOSINSKI: Exactly. This idea grew out of that period of my life, as did *Being There*. By the way, in *Being There*, the protagonist becomes homeless, but he carries no notion of home with him. (laughter)

GIAMO: Do you think that the American ethos would accept the mini-van home for the homeless?

KOSINSKI: I'd like to think that the American ethos would acknowledge it—the Jeffersonian ethos, that is, and I think that if Jefferson were to be here, and I say this with full knowledge of Jefferson's work and his home in Monticello, that he actually would accept it. He would call it going Dutch with the American dream. And it is not an accident that this is the New Amsterdam, and it is not an accident that in Old Amsterdam provisions are made for homeless people. Therefore, if they are made in Old Amsterdam, they should be made in the New Amsterdam.

GIAMO: Would there be an emphasis on mobility with your mini-van home? As you well know, mobility is also very near and dear to the heart of American ideology.

KOSINSKI: In a country in which one-fourth of the people in American

society change homes and become, however temporarily, homeless in between—on the road, if you will—that condition should be accepted as a
given. I think that we must approach the situation from an entirely
American point of view. I think the approach that has emerged to frame
the problem of homelessness is one that has been imposed on the society.
It is an imposition of the welfare state. It's also an approach to the pursuit
of happiness that presupposes that the person should have a home, be
stable, and all kinds of other ingredients which American reality clearly
tells you is not the case. So, then, where is John Dewey and the notion of
the pragmatic American self? Somehow, this has been sacrificed for so
many years.

I think one should reverse it and look at the issue from the most important point of view—and that is from the point of view of the homeless
themselves. How do we make the homeless condition acceptable and,
hence, redeemable and remediable?

G I A M O : Have you done any "market research" on your mini-van home
proposal?

K O S I N S K I : No, it's just now in a design stage of development.

G I A M O : Any "field testing"?

K O S I N S K I : No, but I'm preparing to meet with some architects who
are working on this kind of unit.

G R U N B E R G : By the way, is there any bathroom put into the design of
the unit?

K O S I N S K I : Well, I have no doubt that this could be very easily developed by some manufacturers. These things have been manufactured before. I do not have to point at the objects floating in space left by American astronauts who happened to have been homeless at the time, or am I
not allowed to say this? (laughter)

G I A M O : Basically, what you're saying is that it makes little sense to
attempt small-scale, let alone large-scale, prevention, because prevention

has failed and American ideology will not accept the prevention that might be needed in the cooperative ventures of both public and private sectors to resolve the social problem.

KOSINSKI: Yes, prevention has failed. But we do accept business cycles and recession and unemployment as facts of life. We do accept ruin by bad investments. We do accept crime and being shot at, and we do accept chance. Are we absolutely so deterministically minded that we no longer acknowledge that life is chancy? After all, we do take chances. Therefore, now we live in an ethos in which a homeless person should find far more understanding than in a welfare state. In other words, a person who is right now homeless in front of my home carries within himself or herself all basic American ingredients.

GIAMO: And, whether it's valid or not, some of the homeless do tend to blame themselves for their predicaments.

KOSINSKI: Just as a businessperson might who has invested wrongly. Now if one were to be positive about it, as one should be, and pragmatic, one could improve this condition. Homelessness is very much a part of our American system and, basically, there should be nothing wrong with this condition as long as the individual is not sentenced to unnecessary suffering and punishment—since the system makes all provisions for that condition three miles away downtown in Wall Street.

GRUNBERG: Often, people seem to vacillate between feeling sorry for the homeless or being angry at them. Also, there's a great deal of energy expended in trying to determine who to blame. Is it the homeless individual's fault? Or is it society's fault?

KOSINSKI: These concerns represent non-American values injected into the American character from the outside. They came as the residue of the nineteenth century in its idealized state. And I think one can very easily turn it around. In fact, I think turning it around and improving the lot of a great number of people who now occupy the parking lots at night, and other lots to which they are not entitled, would be far easier than to act against the basic grain of American character.

39

GRUNBERG: So the millions of dollars, the hundreds of millions of dollars that cities are spending in their attempt to rehabilitate, rehouse, feed . . .

KOSINSKI: Work to a degree but, basically, one can also assume that persons who have been homeless carry within them (and we accept it in many other areas of life) a certain philosophy of life or certain experience which makes them, to say the least, apprehensive about ownership. I mean, here's Jerzy Kosinski who is relatively stable (with which most of my literary critics would disagree, judging by my fiction) and who doesn't want to own. Now if I don't want to own a home but prefer to rent one because of my experience of World War II (consider this an experience of homelessness, I repeat that), then why not make a provision for a certain number of people who simply may not be comfortable, or not psychologically or pragmatically equipped anymore, to deal with the state of being rehabilitated, when in fact they may prefer to remain mobile but safe?

GIAMO: How would you distribute these mini-van homes? How would you decide who to give them to?

KOSINSKI: I would leave it flexible, as life itself. And I would say, "Here you are right now. We have no home for you. You may not want one and we are not going to ask you the standard questions. We don't have a home to give you anyway. We want to improve your lot. Now we see you as you are right now. You are without a home; we know that. We have no traditional home for you. Would you like to have one of these mini-vans?" Maybe the question shouldn't even be asked.

Let's try again: "Now, at this point we know that you are a vagrant. There are laws against vagrancy. We can technically arrest you and assign you a home. But, well, we don't have these homes for you either. They happen to be all used up or overcrowded or nonexistent, in case you didn't know that. Now, this means that we are basically leaving you outside of the law. We are, therefore, lawless. The state is lawless; the state should arrest you after midnight. You are a vagrant."

Now, we do have laws about vagrancy. These people should be arrested every night, but they aren't. So the state has failed. Therefore, we should acknowledge that the homeless cannot be legitimately housed, because we are unable or unwilling to do so. It is precisely under these circumstances that I am suggesting that homeless people should be provided tax-deductible, portable, mobile units which fit certain American traditions, such as being on the move.

GRUNBERG: And if they don't take these mobile units, should we arrest them?

KOSINSKI: Well, they will take them. But if they would not take them and then willingly expose themselves to the hazards of nature and fellow humans (far more dangerous than nature itself), then we technically could arrest them on the grounds that they represent a danger to themselves.

GRUNBERG: That raises yet another issue that society seems to have. How far should you go in enforcing your values onto other people, especially if you are not offering them a traditional home?

KOSINSKI: Well, if one wants to be didactic in acting upon this concept (which I'm pursuing firmly enough to pay for the first few hundred thousand of these things myself), one could then teach the homeless several conceptual and organizational skills. First of all, a respect for the traffic, that is, to stay within the established boundaries. Second, the homeless are then organized; they are in a set unit that takes up no more space than necessary. They can no longer expand by adding things to it. Third, it teaches them the notion of home and perhaps for the first time exposes them to the notion that you can be protected by a shelter that is your own and that you are responsible for. It cannot be stolen from you since you are attached to it when you lock yourself in it. It can only be taken with you.

In fact, the mini-van home that I would provide for the homeless takes up much less space than what you see on the streets right now with all the newspapers and bags and everything else. Because some of them are unnecessarily overly affluent, they carry far more than they ought to, while my mobile unit would make them much more realistic. They would take only what they need.

G I A M O: Efficiency—yet another characteristic American value.

K O S I N S K I: Yes, that would also be a prototypical American value, along with mercy, understanding, and pragmatism—all of which this society has excelled in.

G I A M O: Is this how you would go, in the mini-van home, if you were rendered homeless today in New York City?

K O S I N S K I: Absolutely.

G R U N B E R G: So you would stay a protagonist in this manner.

K O S I N S K I: Absolutely. Well, my 1970 Buick performs this function for me now. In a way, it's a vagabond's home. And my trunk is big enough to put a bed in it. Since the Buick is a convertible, the trunk gets the air from the inside of the car. I can sleep in the trunk very easily, and when I lock the trunk, nobody knows I'm there.

G R U N B E R G: Do you still travel with a "comet," that device you described in *The Painted Bird* as a miniature fire-ring, stove, and weapon?

K O S I N S K I: Yes, I do. It is a useful thing to have. That comet in a way is quintessentially what I am trying to do for the homeless. The mobile unit would provide warmth, as you could lie down inside of it, protection from the elements and from attack, and it could go with you.

I talked to every single one of these homeless people—they were black, they were women, they were old, they were young. I said to them, "Listen, if I gave you a cart that could fold into a sleeping compartment, would you use it?" Well, the first thing they asked was "Could it be stolen from me?" But I haven't found a single homeless person who didn't say, "Hey, man, when can I have that?"

G I A M O: But doesn't the mobile home unit, the mini-van concept, go against the American grain in the sense that social reform and personal rehabilitation are being dismissed? It seems like a new form of Hooverville, and don't you think that the public response to this would be negative?

KOSINSKI: Why don't you call it Hoovercraft? We already have a Hovercraft. From Hovercraft to Hoovercraft. A pragmatic society should be able to make that step. (laughter)

GIAMO: But isn't the American tendency to mystify the nature and scope of the social problem?

KOSINSKI: I don't think there is such a thing as an American tendency. I said this in public a long time ago: I like to think that this is the only country, and the only society I know of, that is in a state of a permanent revolution and of a permanent self-redefinition. I think that the mobile home unit should be one of the elements in which this ability of American society can be tested.

GIAMO: But American society has reinvented homelessness for a long period of time—for about 120 years in large urban centers. So it's not a new phenomenon. Yes, it changes, but it also remains the same.

KOSINSKI: Now, since we do make provisions for so many other similar aspects of American society, and since this is a democratic ethos, I see no reason why one should not confront society, or high society if you prefer, precisely with that very ethos that it applies to itself, making provisions for all these conditions that lead to such a state.

GIAMO: Well, in a way, if your proposal does take off, you'll be confronting both the dominant culture of mainstream American society and the marginalized subculture of the homeless. For instance, it's interesting that when the homeless responded to your query they projected a sense of possession into the idea of owning one of these "vehicles": "Can it be stolen?"

KOSINSKI: Absolutely right. Already.

GIAMO: So even though people are down-and-out and living in very,

very harsh conditions (it's not an "official" state of war, but it's probably the closest thing you can get to it in a free society), they still hang on to some values characteristic of the mainstream ethos.

KOSINSKI: Absolutely. No doubt, not to mention life itself. They could very easily commit suicide. Keep in mind that any one of the homeless could find life unbearable. In the very buildings where they sleep there are elevators which would take them to the top floor, to the roof, from which they could jump.

GRUNBERG: So are you saying that the first step the homeless have to take is to assume responsibility for their condition?

KOSINSKI: They already did that. They are alive. They seek food and shelter; the basic conditions of the free enterprise system have been fulfilled.

GIAMO: And this is happening within a context where social responsibility has been abdicated.

KOSINSKI: Absolutely. And the American ethos has been transferred to only downtown and uptown, but not in midtown. By downtown, I mean Wall Street.

GRUNBERG: What is behind this obsession with getting social problems out of sight and out of mind? It seems that communities all around the country are more obsessed with getting the homeless out of their respective areas than they are with examining the suffering that might be going on at their feet.

KOSINSKI: Well, that's fairly understandable, and I can speak only for myself again. I get terribly annoyed when the homeless keep begging. I said to one of them, "Look, what if I give you coupons that I will make so I will know you're the same person I passed three or four times." This way he'll remember that and I can use my extra coupons for some other people.

GRUNBERG: So is it just the bother, the constant interruptions?

KOSINSKI: No doubt. It is, in a way, a form of harassment in our society. Fear is also a factor. Keep in mind that you're not supposed to talk to strangers and suddenly the strangers talk to you. It runs against a certain social behavioral pattern. I have no doubt that, if these issues were to be confronted properly and given additional pragmatic dimensions, even the aspect of begging could be organized as well. These people who beg very often do so under terrible climatic conditions, snow, rain, and the like. So they very cleverly stand (clearly they learn from experience) and bother people who are most bothered by them.

GRUNBERG: They get paid off.

KOSINSKI: Yes, they select the sensitive souls whom they corner. They physically corner them; they bodily corner them, and they say things about their physical conditions which are very unpleasant for most. people to hear. So, in a way, they are paying back to society in the same currency that this society punishes them with.

GIAMO: When I was walking down Fifth Avenue today I saw a blind beggar who had a sign beside him that read: "I am not homeless. I am a blind beggar. I pay my rent." He was differentiating himself in the marketplace of charity.

KOSINSKI: Right. He was trying to join the ethos that he thinks is acceptable. Now there are others, of course, who try to clean your windshield when your wipers can do it.

GRUNBERG: And somehow they don't understand you when you're waving them away. It's like you're waving hello to them.

KOSINSKI: Right, and people are afraid of them because you have to lower your window. Either you are being serviced without payment or you have to pay by lowering your window and exposing yourself to their hands.

GIAMO: Yet some people believe that washing windshields, especially with Windex, is at least a step up from panhandling.

KOSINSKI: But, you see, I feel that this is one of the most humiliating things we do to the homeless. It is most fraudulent on our part to expect them to behave as if they were not beggars and homeless when, in fact, that's precisely what they are.

GRUNBERG: Why is American society not seeing the homeless problem clearly? How many people don't understand the suffering taking place on the streets? And what has allowed for this mystification? The media give people information, but in a fleeting and fragmentary way, and without the deeper knowledge and meaning that is needed. I assume that if most people understood homelessness the way you did, they might awaken to the dimensions of the social problem.

KOSINSKI: If they fully opened themselves up to the existential and pragmatic dimensions of the problem, I think they would become very positive toward it; they would become inventive.

GRUNBERG: Why do you think there has been so little creativity? What is it about American society that isn't working?

KOSINSKI: I think inventiveness has failed. That happens. I think a false sense of predictable life has set in—which is being largely taken away from us. I think that Americans can benefit from some sudden surprises. I look at my 1970 Buick that eats gas that could fuel an airplane. Then I look at my Volkswagen, which I bought in 1969 and keep in Europe. It's a most extraordinary car—a station wagon that almost never needs any gas. Very often I feel that it runs on pure psyche. And it carries four or six individuals and an endless amount of luggage, and it hasn't failed in twenty-two years. Clearly we have technology available. I'm sure that any number of people in business that you talk to, if you were to change their optics, would become inventive again. But this is what I meant about American society. You must come to it with the prodding that stimulates the inventiveness, and that hasn't been done since the middle-class ethos began to bank on the credit card and on the credit system. That's why Detroit lost its status. Detroit had some of the best cars in the world in terms of the overall vehicles, by far the best light, predictable, all-climate, all-road-condition automobiles. But we lost the market to others. Anywhere you look in American society, you find an extraordinary potential that has not been used. The mini-van home is one of them. And that could be a very good test.

G R U N B E R G: We stop; at some point we stop.

K O S I N S K I: Yes, we stop. It's that stopping mechanism at work.

G R U N B E R G: You have talked about the effects of television before. Once I read one of your interviews and you discussed how television promotes this kind of stopping.

K O S I N S K I: Yes, by rendering people to the level of spectators, totally passive, and no longer able to provide images from within. Imagination, therefore, is torpedoed. Everything is given and it's a totalitarian medium; you are not in charge of the images. They're not yours, so the only thing you can do is take it or leave it.

But there's another ingredient. Television reinforces some of the static values by repeating them and multiplying them from day to day. If you watch television, on the average for six or seven hours a day now in America, you see people with homes and with cars so often that you cannot imagine someone actually being homeless. The homeless appear on the TV screen much less frequently than they appear in your life. In your life, especially if you live in a large city, you see them practically nonstop. But it is the television that you watch much more often and for a much longer period of time. To find out what the weather is, you turn not to your window but to your TV set. Hence all you need is one imaginative television program, or one protagonist played by an attractive actor, to catch people's attention. Instead of showing Hughes the millionaire, why not get Warren Beatty to play an imaginative hobo—a hobo from Hoboken. You would get then a sudden understanding, because the exposure of that protagonist would be so much greater than the intellectual thesis that we are trying to develop around it. There is no prototypical figure that you can point your finger at. In life, yes, but in life you pass this person by. You dismiss this person by using an old-fashioned ethos, or a rigid predicament of your own, that makes no provision for someone who is vomiting on the sidewalk in front of the bank. And this is a bank, mind you, which issues you the card called MasterCharge, and here is a human being neither a master nor in charge sleeping in front of the bank that should have the charge to take care of this person. This means that basically you disregard it altogether.

So you truly need either a great cartoon or a television program in which this condition could be portrayed in all the dimensions that we have just mentioned: suddenly acceptable, understandable, profoundly humane and touching, and eminently redeemable without sacrifice that cannot be made; hence, one more condition—realistic.

GRUNBERG: So *Hill Street Blues* plus *Sanford and Sons*.

KOSINSKI: See, you said it. I would gladly play in it. With my three minutes in *Reds*, I am perfectly equipped for the part . . . (laughter)

Now, I honestly believe, because I love this country, that all the understanding for this concept and proposal is here. It is implicit in the American character. It is available on every street corner of American life. But you've got to be pragmatic about it, and everyone I have met so far comes to this as a foreigner, speaking the language of Saint-Simon and utopian villages in which houses are given for nothing—all of the fraudulent language of Stalin. That is the old American left that somehow made its fraudulent way into the American character, saying, "We must, we must. We are rich. We are well-to-do. We are eating steaks and these people are eating from the garbage cans. They should have filet mignon at least once a week too."

GRUNBERG: And that's enough, like the big Thanksgiving dinners they have for the homeless once a year.

KOSINSKI: That's it, and, of course, all this to make my life easier so I can rest in my triplex without any bad dreams.

GRUNBERG: So, with this vision of yours, are we going to head toward the ruling class living in penthouses and everyone else in these little mobile homes?

KOSINSKI: I think we are moving very rapidly toward a time in American history, and I think it's going to be very positive, where an ultimate dream for an American businessperson would be to get one of these mobile carts and gain so much productive time. (laughter)

GIAMO: You could work until midnight everyday and increase your productivity tenfold. (laughter)

KOSINSKI: You could see the ads for it: "In any neighborhood you choose! Buy your own groceries! Be free from crime!" . . . (laughter)

GIAMO: In the introduction to the Houghton Mifflin second edition of *The Painted Bird*, you recounted your experience of switching from social science writing to fiction writing.

KOSINSKI: Yes.

GRUNBERG: But we get the feeling that you never really left the social sciences.

KOSINSKI: Well, it's not the social sciences; I think it has to do with exercising your societal being. It's a condition imposed on my generation probably by the realization that childhood is a state of war. Now add to that the experience of a real war; it is the child who suffers first. Normally the child is at war with the grownups. But, during a real war, the child or youth is at war with the grownups as well as with the other grownups who are taking their grownups away—their mothers and fathers. So, because of this, I think that most of my generation has been far more conscious of society as a foreign phenomenon and as a force that can be very hostile and brutal. But we are also very bureaucratically minded. For instance, I like to think that two bureaucrats constitute a democratic effort, and this could be a remedial force that forces the rich and the poor to stay in the same lane.

SISTER MARY ROSE McGEADY, D.C.

The Common Good

JEFFREY GRUNBERG: In this day and age, what is a religious perspective?

SISTER MARY ROSE McGEADY: Well, a religious perspective is a faith perspective. It acknowledges that we are responsible for one another. It is the understanding that we are all brothers and sisters. As an institution, the church sees itself as responsible for promoting this view and for organizing it. It's not a question of proselytizing; it's really one of care. It's the human element raised to the dimension of faith.

BENEDICT GIAMO: You were also trained as a psychologist. Did you find any conflicts between your training as a psychologist and your training in the religious faith as a Daughter of Charity?

McGEADY: When I was young, there were times when I used to sit and ponder certain questions. I no longer find any conflicts.

GIAMO: What major conflict did you struggle with when you were young?

McGEADY: I think probably the whole concept of determinism. You know, when you study determinism in psychology and you think: "Am I determined or am I free? What is really true? Is determinism really a concept?" How do we put that together with the whole dimension of faith that says God is our Father, that He gives us free will, and that He cares for each and every one of us? And how do we reconcile the notion of determinism with the following precepts: God is involved in our lives; nothing happens to us by accident; it's all part of the plan of God? We believe that He plans only good things for us and yet we see so many bad things happening. It's the whole good and evil issue. By the way, I haven't solved that one.

GRUNBERG: So are you saying that cause becomes unimportant? What caused this person to be doing drugs? A weakness in character? Did God choose him or her to suffer in this way?

McGEADY: I don't think God ever plans evil. I think that God put in every person the ability to make decisions. And much of what is evil in our world today is a result of human decisions which visit evil in other peoples' lives. God gives us the freedom to choose. If people choose to do things that cause problems for other people, then that's a human decision; that's not God's decision. And yet He doesn't take away that freedom to choose. If He were to take away that freedom so that we could not make evil decisions, then we would have lost our free will—and that's probably the greatest gift we have. It's true that there is a lot of suffering in this world. Of course, there are natural disasters. *But there are very few pieces of human suffering* that you can't trace back to human decision making. The whole drug issue is an example. Many human decisions, free choices by people, continue to contribute to the drug trade.

GIAMO: And I would think that the matrix of decision making gets more and more intricate with more far-reaching consequences for people.

MCGEADY: It's because of the smallness of the world. It's true now that some person can make a decision that has repercussions for millions of peoples' lives. Years ago, that would have been less likely because the world was not so small. Therefore, to be honest with you, I feel that there are many holes in our social fabric. Much of what held our society together has been disintegrating. I still think that there's a great deal of human goodness and many people who really care, for religious or for humanitarian reasons. There are a lot of caring people in the world, and I think they replace many of the structures, such as the family and the church, that used to hold our society together.

GIAMO: With these dual perspectives of religion and psychology in mind, how does your approach differ from that of the Catholic Worker, whose approach, as I understand it, is to minister to the basic needs of food, shelter, and clothing, without any systematic attention given to intervention and rehabilitation?

MCGEADY: I think the major difference would be that my philosophy, and, therefore, my stance in terms of services, would be geared much more toward rehabilitation. I believe that all people have the right to be developed to their fullest potential. In whatever ways we work with other people it should not be just to meet the basic necessities, but to help people as far as we can to meet their potential. I think that this approach is very much characteristic of the various programs at Covenant House. Although some people see what we do as simply providing food, clothing, and shelter, in fact, it's a whole lot more. I believe "the glory of God is man/woman fully alive!"

GIAMO: Was this shift in philosophy a historic change within the social services arm of the church, that is, to move from the ministering services offered by the Catholic Worker to the rehabilitative services that Covenant House provides?

MCGEADY: I don't think so. To be honest with you, I don't know enough about the Catholic Worker to critique it well, although I did meet Dorothy Day when I was in Rhinebeck running a psychiatric treatment center for disturbed children. Dorothy was in Tivoli, a town up the road, running her farm, and she came to me one day with a little boy who was the child of one of their farm workers. He was clearly schizophrenic, and Dorothy asked my opinion. I strongly recommended that Dorothy get professional help for the child. She thought that by just changing this child's environment, by bringing him to the farm, he would get better. Dorothy was very humble and very open with me, and she said, "It doesn't seem to be working; what do you think?" So I spent some time with the child and told Dorothy right off that it was very clear to me that this was a schizophrenic child, maybe even an autistic child, and that she needed to seek professional help. Dorothy told me that she brought the child back to the city and got him help. I believe that Dorothy Day would have agreed that human development was a part of charity, of true love. Maybe she believed that human development would take place best in the atmosphere of community living and the outdoors. It is just a different approach.

GIAMO: From what I understand, I think it's very close to what you just mentioned—the community aspect, and the total receptivity to people.

MCGEADY: And the community that was formed in the Catholic

Worker was really the ingredient where help was most likely to take place. The human support and the feeling that there were other people who cared made all the difference.

GIAMO: Does the church have an official position on the problem of homelessness?

McGEADY: Well, the pope has a document on homelessness. It's about five years old now, and I had it when I was in Brooklyn working for Catholic Charities two years ago. The document was out for a couple of years before I knew about it, and I was working with the homeless at the time. You could have written it, or I could have written it; it's very much a document that deals with the social reality and the responsibility that we all have for one another. It also deals with the need for social policy. Taking its concepts and promoting social policy is the most powerful thing that the church is committed to today. The reason for the Vatican document on homelessness was to provide a guide for the bishops, who then formed state conferences where the really hard work developing social policy occurred. There was also a document on homelessness that I helped to write for the New York State Catholic Conference. The church works in layers, so that when a document comes out of the Vatican, much is already going on at lower levels. But it's always good when we get something from the top that greases those wheels, so that someone who might not have been so proactive in terms of social policy is more willing to enter the fray. The problem with homelessness is that it's always been there, hasn't it? But I think we're calling many other things homelessness now.

GRUNBERG: It has become a big umbrella term, hasn't it?

McGEADY: Yes. And, you know, there's still a kind of magical thinking that, if we do something, homelessness will go away. And that's just false. There's no one thing that we can do to get rid of homelessness; we have to do many, many things to handle the problem. When I look at our kids here at Covenant House, I see two vicious cycles. I see what has been the insidiously vicious cycle that leads from poverty to family conflict to family collapse and ultimately to the displacement of family members. That cycle continues. Then you have the new cycle that's complicating life, that is, the cycle in our modern society that is oriented toward materialism and success and the acquisition of things—of money. Thus, the poor kid, especially the poor adolescent, who wants to have the material things and wants money can be led very easily into the drug industry. And we use the word "industry" because we see kids who have worked in every phase of that industry, from being lookouts and runners to sellers and buyers. And then they get lured into prostitution as a way of getting money to buy drugs. I feel it's very hard to be a kid today, especially a kid in a poor family. A poor family has to be super strong to survive these days.

GIAMO: In light of your comment about the permanence of homelessness over time, would you please clarify Matthew 26:6–13 in which, forseeing the passion, Jesus was anointed by the woman in Bethany in anticipation of his burial? As you know, Jesus took a lot of heat from his apostles for wasting precious oils that could have been sold, with the proceeds distributed to the poor. And, in the frequently quoted phrase, Jesus replied to his apostles: "Why do you trouble the woman? She has done me a good turn, for the poor you have always with you but you do not always have me."

MCGEADY: Well, for me, what those words mean is that the woman was really performing an act of love for God, and she saw Jesus as the Messiah. She was doing more than performing a human act. I think Jesus was really saying this too—paying homage to God—must be part of human activity.

To understand this passage you have to take the whole Gospel into consideration. In Matthew 25, Jesus talks about giving food to the hungry and drink to the thirsty: "And whatsoever you do to the least of my brothers you do unto me." So that we serve God in two ways. We serve Him by our *worship*, which to me is the real meaning of Jesus' anointing by the woman in Bethany, and by *service*. It is important to understand the totality of His message. I think that "the poor you have always with you" was not a putdown on the poor at all. You must take this phrase and apply it to the other places in the Gospels where He talks about service. And I think the most powerful line in the scriptures is this: "Whatever you do, you do unto me." This raises charity to an act of worship of God, and, if we really believe what is in the Gospel, then we believe that God resides in each of us, in every person who is alive. That's why the church has always had the big missionary push to search for the poor, to find them and to serve them. What's happening now is "the hurrier we go the behinder we get." The problem of human need outstrips our capacity to deal with it.

The church has a much different missionary thrust than it once had. It's almost overwhelmed by the social problems that we face today. We have people sitting in the pews of our churches who have real difficulty coping with the answer to the question "What is the degree of your responsibility?" They have real problems with that. "Is it enough to give money?" "Is this giving of money a sufficient act of religion?" "Do we have to give of ourselves in order to feel that we've served our brothers and sisters?" Whether we act in direct service or by giving money, the church continues to preach the responsibility that we have to one another. The problem is that the church has multiplied its social agencies almost exhaustively, and it's having real difficulty keeping up with the many claims on its attention. As pluralism became more acceptable in society and in the church, and as public funding was given to religious organizations, the typical person in the pew began to feel less responsible. The attitude "Let the government do it" has become much more of a danger to the historic mission of the church.

GRUNBERG: So the poor will always be with us?

MCGEADY: The poor will always be with us in the sense that there will always be some people who just don't fare as well as other people. Even within an ideal society, you will always have mental illness, retardation, the elderly and disabled, the sick, and people unable to make it on their own.

GRUNBERG: Peter Berger, a sociologist, wrote a book called *The Homeless Mind*. In the book he says that, from a sociological perspective, religion is a structure that makes it possible for humankind to feel at home in the universe. He discusses how religion has left the public forum and has become more privatized than ever before. It's up to each individual. Insofar as the institution of religion has diminished (it isn't "out there" so much to help us feel at home anymore), do you think that homelessness signals a deepening spiritual crisis in this country?

MCGEADY: What's going through my mind now is our recent Midnight Mass with Monsignor William Toohy. His sermon at Midnight Mass stressed that, as a result of Christmas, nobody ever needs to feel homeless again. We should all have a sense of belonging, and the coming of Jesus into human form was the merger of the Godhead with humanity so that all of us now belong. We should all feel that we have a home. That's what your question brought to mind immediately. I would have to think about Berger's concept. But to the extent that homelessness represents a loss of caring, of feeling responsible on the part of people, yes, it is a spiritual or faith crisis.

GIAMO: "Rock of Ages, cleft for me, / Let me hide myself in Thee" also comes to mind.

MCGEADY: Yes, and I feel in a way that we're talking about one another too when we talk about home in a more philosophical sense. See, I feel that more important than home is the sense of belonging. And I think the most desperate situation in life for anyone, whether an individual has a roof over her head or not, is the feeling that there's nobody in the world who cares. The most significant statistic in Covenant House is that 25 percent of our kids cannot give us a name or a number to call in an emergency. When I questioned one girl about that, she said there's nobody to call. And I said, "You don't have a grandmother? Or a brother? Or an aunt? Suppose you get hit by a car and are in the hospital and we don't know if you're going to live or die and we want to let somebody know." She looked me right in the eye and said, "Sister, if that ever happens just pray for me 'cause there ain't nobody on this earth who gives a damn if I live or die." Now, to me, that's homelessness—because the sense of belonging is gone. They are disconnected from meaningful, caring, and loving relationships.

When we deal with our kids, people ask me all the time, how much do you succeed? And I say, maybe with 40 percent of the kids we succeed in getting them off the streets and into something that is a more stable environment by our social standards. But when do we really succeed? I think we really succeed in those cases when the kid comes to us at the point where he hasn't any sense of belonging left; there is literally nobody on the face of the earth that this kid feels he belongs to, even if there's an address someplace. When he has reached this point of total vulnerability or defenselessness, he will let us move in and help. To be alone out there in this big, horrible world is terrifying; then, without even saying it, he permits us to help. And we become at least *pro tem* that sense of belonging. The kids *belong* to Covenant House.

GRUNBERG: It's a rapprochement that you have as an adolescent with your parents. You leave them but then you return. If they don't have that, then they can't return.

McGEADY: Yes, you know I do this often when I talk to the staff. I often say that Covenant House is only as good as the quality in us. When any staff member—the guard, the cook, the social worker, the psychiatrist—touches the kid, then there exists the potential to create a link. And that link is what Covenant House is all about. Giving a kid a sense of linkage, somebody who really cares and who's not just collecting a paycheck, results in that difficult to define thing we call a relationship. And that is the essence of Covenant House—to reconnect the kids who have become disconnected from society. If we want to keep these kids from becoming homeless over the next thirty years, then the prevention rests in the processes of reconnection.

GIAMO: You have a program called Rights of Passage. How does this help to rebuild the connections?

McGEADY: That's our "after the crisis" shelter. In the Crisis Shelter, we get thirty to sixty new kids a day. Some of them stay, some of them don't. We tell them they have to give up their weapons and drugs in order to stay overnight, and some of them walk back out. But for the kids who stay in that Crisis Shelter, very little pressure is put on them, very few expectations. We only expect that they give up their drugs and their guns, and that they don't fight. They can stay for a few days or a few weeks, until they get their act together. Then we begin case management. And that's when they move into the Rights of Passage program. These are kids who were really left high and dry, with no place to go, nothing to connect to. So this program really begins the rehabilitation process.

GIAMO: So then you take them through a meaningful series of activities.

McGEADY: Yes. The easy cases for us are those kids who have families who really want them. For example, there is the kid who had a fight with his father over the car. They cursed at each other, and the father said, "Get out of here; if you don't like the rules in this house, then get out." That happens a million times a day in the good old U.S.A.

And we get calls on our hot line 24 hours a day: "My father threw me out; what do I do next?" Those kids are the easy ones, because we can mediate the situation. We can be the buffer that creates the first contact back to good old dad who, by the way, is worried to death about where his kid is but won't tell him so. Those are our easy cases. But the difficult cases are the kids who have no one to connect with out there. I said to one kid, "How did you land here?" And he said, "Well, I don't know where my father is; he's been gone a long time, and they arrested my mother last month for selling drugs and she's in Rikers Island [a New York City prison]. I'm 16 and my sister is 15. The cops just left us in the apartment and nobody did anything about us. We knew that as soon as the landlord found out that we were minors he would kick us out, so my sister and I were scared to death; thank God our friends knew about Covenant House." Talk about homelessness in our society. We have a child care system in this country, but the typical adolescent has a really hard time fitting into a system that attempts to put him in a foster home or in a possible adoption. It's too scary for the kid who is newly disenfranchised. So when we have a 16-year-old kid, we have our hands full, because, legally, we have to turn a kid over to the child welfare administration, and he doesn't want to go. And for the child welfare administration to find a home for a 16-year-old kid, especially a minority kid, is very difficult. So we report them, but often the kids stay here because there just isn't anything out there for them. The systems are just not adequate, and adolescents are just not welcome in as many places.

In our Rights of Passage program every kid has a volunteer mentor. Most of these volunteers are from the business community, and many of them, both men and women, are well off and very successful. We ask them to just be there for the kids: advisor, buddy, a kind of parent. We ask them to give four hours per week to the youngster. It can be an hour and a half on the phone; it can be lunch or supper; it can be just a car ride or a walk down the river.

They can ask their mentors: "What do you think about this? What do you think about that?" Without realizing it, they're getting substitute parenting. And the mentors? When we train the mentors we tell them not to make decisions for the kids, but to lay out all the options for them, because our kids' experiences are so limited they don't know the options. "Don't make a decision too fast. Have you thought about this? Have you thought about that?" Mentors sit and talk to the kids as if they were real people. They don't just order them around, and so it's different from the kids' relationship to prior teachers and counselors. The kids tell us that this mentoring relationship is the best part of the Rights of Passage program.

GRUNBERG: In Friedrich Nietzsche's preface to *The Genealogy of Morals*, he wrote that "we have no right to be disconnected." Of course, he went on to explore what is good and evil and how we come to these terms. In light of Nietzsche's assertion, do you think that the poverty of homelessness is morally wrong?

MCGEADY: Well, the origin of the word "moral" is *mores*, which means custom or expectation. It's like the mind of the body politic. In modern parlance the use of the word "moral" implies an action that is praiseworthy or blameworthy. And I think there are actions, such as evictions, that are blameworthy. But to take the whole problem of homelessness and call it moral or immoral, as though some action, some one person's action created it, is like going on a wild goose chase to hold someone responsible. It's the body politic that is acting in an immoral way. If we believed that we are responsible for our more vulnerable brothers and sisters, which, by the way, was a key thought in the foundation of this country—the responsibility of the whole to the individual—then the body politic would be acting differently than it is today. I think that social responsibility has eroded in our contemporary society. People have a hard time reconciling their own desires to live comfortably with their responsibility to the poor. So, to look upon the totality of it, I think that homelessness poses a moral situation in the sense that it's a whole collection of individual decisions which are morally culpable. Homelessness is morally wrong because it is the result of many individual decisions or lack of decisions.

GRUNBERG: So can a country then have a soul?

McGEADY: I think a nation can have a conscience and needs to have a conscience. But that conscience should really be the *corporate* conscience, the conscience that comes out of all the individual consciences. So, putting us all together, if you have a conscience and I have a conscience, then all of us form a corporate conscience that can tell us what is right and what is wrong. And historically in our nation we have had a corporate conscience and consciousness that judged certain things, like the care of the widow and the orphan which goes back to the scriptures. It tells us to take care of the widow and the orphan. Where did that come from? It came from an innate sense of what's right and wrong. I believe that there is an innate sense of right and wrong. It is sometimes called the natural law. The concept of the common good is very much in jeopardy in this nation. I don't think that as a nation we're coming to a clear vision of the common good—that each individual must subjugate his or her own desires and needs in order to contribute to the common good. Perhaps people have to sacrifice. I often think, why is there such enormous resistance to increasing taxation? More public funding is a solution to our social dilemmas, but we are losing this concept of the common good—the notion that I can only live comfortably to the extent that I am willing to contribute to the common good, to my brothers and sisters who are not able on their own to live a decent life.

GIAMO: Has the achievement of affluence replaced the more traditional and spiritual achievement of goodness as our chief pursuit, and is this shift from sacred to secular forms of aspiration part of the erosion of the common good?

McGEADY: It's almost as if we have two instincts, both of which can be good. One is the instinct for self-aggrandizement, for personal wealth and the desire to possess material goods. And then there's this conscience that drives us to feel responsible for other people. I think this creates a huge conflict in people. People write to me all the time and say here's my $10 check; I wish it were more, but I'm so afraid of war and I'm so afraid of this or that. People are terribly insecure, even with what they've got in our society. In terms of the young people, they see so much of society's materialism emphasized on television, which says to them: "You're not a person unless you've got a lot of stuff." Kids feel useless because they don't feel successful. The self-concepts of our kids are so miserable that it just makes you want to cry. There are very, very few kids here (at Covenant House) who feel good about themselves. It comes usually from a lack of achievement, a feeling that they haven't done anything. There's very little concept of who I am, or how good I am, or the good thoughts that I have, or the friendly things that I do for other people. Being worthwhile in our society is so tied in people's minds to what they've got or what they've done, not to what they are.

GIAMO: And the standards for achievement—for the good life—are sometimes very dubious. For instance, I was coming into the city the other night and I was struck by an image of a homeless man selling his meager wares on the Upper West Side of Manhattan. He was on the sidewalk and in the background and above him was a montage of posters, one of which was an advertisement for Madonna and her new album, "The Immaculate Collection." What is the *measure* of success in our society when Madonna is the image, you might say the secular Madonna, for the achievement of status, sexuality, wealth, privilege, and power? And in the foreground you have this barely surviving homeless man who represents failure to all of society. Who is really worthy of reverence in that particular situation?

MCGEADY: The whole world's turned upside down. The whole world is screwy!

GIAMO: Does the growing problem of extreme poverty and homelessness reconstitute the problem of evil in modern life? By evil, I mean man's inhumanity to man.

MCGEADY: Yes, I think it does, I really do. I still say that you can call poverty by a lot of different names and different words, but the basic problem is that we have a very large segment of our population that is in dire need. I see homelessness as a problem in itself, but I also view it as a symptom of other social problems, such as family breakdown. Even if we attack homelessness from one point of view, such as housing, we will continue to have a homeless population emerging because the family constellation is breaking down, the sense of belonging is eroding. I think that American culture has lost sight of a sense of what's right and what's wrong. How can you call something evil unless you have a concept that it's wrong? That's where I think there is the greatest deterioration in moral values, or even the word—"values"—period. If our highest value is respect for one another—respect for God first and then respect for one another as brothers and sisters, children of God, then that creates expectations in terms of the decisions we make in our lives about what's right and what's wrong. Many people have just stopped demanding these things of themselves. They wait to be told what's right and what's wrong. If you really think about the implications of this and you make these judgments, it's almost too scary; it's easier to walk away.

GRUNBERG: What problems do homeless women face? Now, I know that shelters for homeless women overlap with shelters for battered women. This doesn't say a whole lot about the chances for the children involved, does it?

MCGEADY: No. We have a growing population of women with children coming to Covenant House. Many of them will never get over the fact that they were too young to be parents. They are forced into the responsibilities of parenting and adulthood before they are developmentally ready. I believe homeless women often have their situation complicated by a number of problems: no or poor prior work experience, no job skills, children—either with them or in foster care.

GRUNBERG: How important is it to locate the fathers or the mothers of your Covenant House runaway children? Do you spend a lot of time trying to reconnect the family members?

MCGEADY: In terms of the parental relationship, we are very dependent upon what the kids tell us. We don't spend much time looking for parents that the kids have written off. But we don't make that decision for a while. We really spend a lot of time talking to a kid about whether or not anyone is really "out there" for her, because we believe that re-creating that family connection is critically important where possible. We often play the role of negotiator or mediator with parents to ask that they give a kid a second chance. And usually we are successful.

There are some kids that can be in touch with their parents by picking up the phone, but opt not to because they feel so rejected or so hurt. Sometimes, as the kids get older, they begin to see that parents—not just themselves—also have problems. In fact, they can almost become parents to the parent. But it takes a lot of psychological distance in order to do that. So, yes, we try very hard to recreate any relationships with any fragment of family life because we think it's the *sine qua non*. If there is a connecting fragment, a sense of belonging—"somebody out there belongs to me"—then that can make all the difference in the world. Also, we often try to recreate relationships with siblings who may be in foster care. We have many kids who graduate from foster care. I'm being selective when I say this, but the foster care system is graduating an awful lot of disconnected kids. Over 50 percent of our kids here at Covenant House have been in foster care. What does that statistic mean? It means that the family broke down a long time ago. We have kids who talk of being in nine foster homes and they'll joke, "Oh, I got kicked out of five of them and I ran away from two." We have runaway kids in our shelter who came from foster homes, because they don't feel like a part of the family; they feel like they're being put up with; they feel like they're the ones who get picked on and blamed for everything.

GIAMO: How many kids are on the road on any given night?

MCGEADY: Only God knows. Only God knows. Estimates are all we have. Some say a million nationwide.

GRUNBERG: In 1987, of the intact families (families that became homeless and one or both parents are still there) the statistics showed there were 100,000 homeless children on any given night. Now, that doesn't include runaways, stowaways, or abandoned kids.

McGEADY: I was out at our Covenant House in Los Angeles a few weeks ago. For the first time in my life, on Los Angeles' skid row, I saw homeless women sitting on the pavement with little children around them. I've never seen that before, even in New York. Is there anything sadder than seeing little children growing up living on the street? It is pathetic.

We experience this situation because we've housed a lot of young mothers with babies who live with their boyfriends for a while, or are used by someone else, and then they get put out and are really homeless. But, actually, to see young mothers look like that, raising their kids on the streets—it's terribly, terribly distressing.

GRUNBERG: I wanted to ask you a question about advocates. Advocates are essential whenever there is suffering. However, there is a danger that advocates can become overly politicized and simplistic in their rhetoric and program for social action, often to the detriment of the people whose cause they are claiming to champion. In light of this, how do you view the mission of advocates?

McGEADY: Philosophically, it's the difference between *doing for* and *doing with* poor people. When you keep the people for whom you are advocating involved, then your chances of being a true advocate are much better. But when you become the authority on how to solve their problems *without* involving them, then advocacy fails. And there's a terrible temptation for the professionals in this country to think that they know—a real "father knows best" approach. But when you involve the people themselves in the process, then you find out your limitations. In fact, I think it's very important for me to keep talking with the kids. By talking *with* the victims, not just *about* them, we come much closer to truth, and as advocates we must deal with *truth*! Whenever I visit a program, I meet with the director, I meet with the board, I meet with the staff, and I meet with the kids. And I say to the kids, "What do you think about this place?" And the last question I've been asking them concerns drugs: "Do we need to do more to help those of you involved with drugs?" And although I tell them that I'm not after any true confessions, invariably that's what I get. The drug problem has so permeated teenage culture that it is now a rarity for any kid not to have been involved in some aspect of the drug culture. And it's a vicious cycle. Step down into poverty in our society and the likelihood is that you'll eventually step into the drug culture; it's the fastest way to make money. Then you also step into prostitution and crime. It's almost a guarantee.

GIAMO: And, as you mentioned earlier, you feel that the emphasis on materialism is what's driving this vicious cycle.

MCGEADY: Absolutely. Money and things are the realities behind the power of the drug industry and its attraction for the poor.

GRUNBERG: There doesn't seem to be any way out of that for society. It's certainly not diminishing.

MCGEADY: No, it's getting worse. It's insidious. I feel that it's almost impossible to keep inculcating values into kids while they're so caught up in all this. It's like banging your head against a brick wall. You know, if we could add to the school curriculum, I would teach self-esteem exercises from kindergarten up. I think kids need so much affirmation, and they need affirmation for doing *the human thing*, the right thing. Not for beating up all the other kids, not for winning, but simply for doing the human thing. Kids need reinforcement for being kind and helpful to each other. The saddest group for us to deal with is the 17-, 18-, and 19-year-olds who feel that they're worthless. "I don't even know why you bother with me." They often say that about themselves. And, I'll tell you, we live here with our eyes open all the time because we have so much potential suicide on our hands.

GRUNBERG: Is there something wrong then with our vision of society? Or is it a matter of policy?

MCGEADY: It's both. If I could change policies in this country, I would change about a thousand of them.

GRUNBERG: What comes to mind first?

MCGEADY: Well, I think we need a family policy in this country. We need to come up with ways to really support families so we don't keep creating generation after generation of families who are locked into poverty. Therefore, I would like some kind of subsistence wage paid to families who can only earn the minimum wage. You can't live on the minimum wage. Therefore, I would like either a higher minimum wage or some form of subsistence given to the working poor that would motivate them to work. Then they would have the potential to attain a higher standard of living. As I said before, work is critical to how we all think about ourselves, our self-worth and self-esteem. At Covenant House we try hard to instill this in the kids.

We don't have any family policies in this country. We also need day care. We're on the verge of better day care policy, but it will probably be too little even if it is passed. I think housing policy is a crying need, and I think the worst thing the Reagan Administration did to this country was kill housing development. Even when you get people on their feet, you can't get them into decent housing. There's so many millions of people living in criminally substandard housing in this nation.

G I A M O: Is there any form of political government that would be aligned with your vision of the good society?

M c G E A D Y: I think our system of government could realize the good society—if self-interest and selfishness were checked. Last night, on the news, I heard there probably won't be a vote in Congress on the possibility of war in the Persian Gulf, because the Republicans are afraid that if the vote takes place and it isn't successful, it would look bad for them. The Democrats, in contrast, don't want to vote because they want to push the whole responsibility of this potential war on the Republicans. That's all self-interest. That's not the common good; that's not the public interest, is it? I think this is the core of the conflict. Self-interest and selfishness have become so ingrained, especially in our political process, that we can no longer expect the common good to be satisfied. How do we reconvert this nation to taking the high road in terms of the common good?

G I A M O: What will it take to restore that sense of the common good?

M c G E A D Y: If I knew the answer to that I could run for president.

GIAMO: Do we need a miracle?

McGEADY: We need many miracles. Way back, a priest gave a talk to the National Conference of Catholic Charities and he said, "What do we need to do? Do we need to change systems? Or do we need to change people's hearts?" Well, we need to do both. It's not a simple issue, because you don't do either one of those things easily. But I often say to myself, "Why do people send their dollars to Covenant House? Why do people give?" We got 187,000 pieces of mail over the Christmas holidays. Some of them with a dollar and one with $100,000. I believe that thinking people, caring people, are looking at our society and are very unhappy with what they see. Everybody feels so helpless, because the problem has become so big, so multifaceted. Yet they feel that *they should do something*. So they look around and they find an organization they think is doing something good. And they put their concern in an envelope and they send it to a place like Covenant House, or the Red Cross, or the Salvation Army.

GIAMO: It doesn't make any systemic changes—or perhaps little permanent change in one's own heart, but it does offer some support, a vote of confidence in your direction.

McGEADY: I think they're saying: "I feel responsible and I'm trying to live out my responsibilities. I've got to do *something*. So I'm going to do something to help somebody I think is doing something about the situation in our country." That's my interpretation of what's happening.

GIAMO: But at bottom there's a sense of desperation and helplessness. It is very complex, living in America.

McGEADY: Oh yes, but I tell you, I have a hard job but I also have a lot of hope, because I see so much goodness. We've got many problems in this nation, but we also have an awful lot of goodness. I get letters in scratchy handwriting: "I'm 88 years old and I thank God my kids made it and I have nice grandchildren. But I'm worried about my grandchildren and I'm sending you this $50 to help the kids." There's so much of that in this nation, in the midst of all these problems, you just have to keep the two balls up in the air and try to keep them from bouncing off one another.

GIAMO: It's the classic confrontation with good and evil—always at war with each other.

McGEADY: Absolutely.

GIAMO: Obviously, you see capacities for both.

McGEADY: Yes, I guess I would be really depressed if I only saw the problems increasing and I saw people's hearts shutting down. Even with our kids—some of them have grown aloof; they've tried everything, and yet when you get them into a decent living situation, you can begin to touch the goodness in them. We have our kids going down to the soup kitchen on 8th Avenue and volunteering. It brings a smile around here—our kids are working in a soup kitchen! But we're trying to teach them to give and not just to take.

Part 2

The Public Interest

HAZEL DUKES

Advocacy and Leadership

JEFFREY GRUNBERG: Let's start right off by asking how you view the problem of homelessness in today's society.

HAZEL DUKES: I believe personally that a home is not all a person needs. It should not be simplified to that point. The homeless need support services for a while until they feel that they can cope with other problems. For example, if all a person has is $300, she will need to make a budget out of that. You know, if you only have ten tokens for the week, you plan accordingly. You know you have to pay the light bill or the lights are going to be turned off.

BENEDICT GIAMO: How do problems get simplified to the point where critical issues don't get resolved in ways that are really helpful?

DUKES: Let me answer this way. I worked with a poverty program associated with the National Board of Economic Opportunity. I always told the social workers that I wanted them to become more than just social workers. I wanted them to become visionaries for every family they worked with. Whenever I went to a home, I found that the wife or the husband had some leadership or thinking ability. I always went back to the social worker and said that, when we meet with this family, we have to talk about jobs, about the future of their children, about stabilizing the family. But we do have to start with day care, because in order to keep this family stabilized both parents need to go to work; so they have to be able to put their children in a safe place.

One of the qualities we have lost is the time to let social workers be social workers. They really only have time to do maintenance work. They repair, but there is nobody to sit with the family and work with the family's strengths. I spoke to social workers at Harlem Hospital about a month ago and I told them that they have to get back to being activists; they have to get back to the street.

GIAMO: When you talk about the community, I'm reminded that, historically, the strongest institutions within the inner cities have been religion and family. What role does each play today?

GRUNBERG: And let me add that in New York City the average age of homeless people is getting younger and younger, and the overwhelming majority of the homeless population is black, with as many single men as broken families. What has happened to the relationship between the institutions of church and family and young black males?

DUKES: When I go into a prison to talk to these young men, I ask them, "Who's your pastor? What church are you affiliated with?" But they have no answer. They came from the "now" generation and didn't want to hear about religious institutions. They belonged to young parents who had strayed from or who had rebelled against religious institutions, so they never experienced that foundation.

GIAMO: These institutions then are not part of their experience?

DUKES: No, they're not. And their grandmothers are young. When you have kids having babies at 14, 15, and 16, the grandmother then is in her late 20s, and she doesn't have these values.

GRUNBERG: James Baldwin once wrote of himself as "a kind of bastard of the West" ["Autobiographical Notes" (1955) in *Notes of a Native Son*]; that he had been rendered marginal—neither a member of the dominant class of white American society nor a "citizen" of Africa. Within this context of identity and belonging, one could generalize and argue that African Americans were homeless to begin with. What is your outlook on this?

DUKES: Well, that is debatable. I was born in Montgomery, Alabama. Rosa Parks lived right down the block from me. I understood early in my life who I was because I had black teachers who lived in my community and who also taught at my Sunday school. When I look back, and I believe in integration, I think that most southern blacks—like the Andy Youngs and the Martin Luther Kings—wouldn't know about this concept of basic homelessness as you describe it. We had a greater sense of who we were; we *had* a homeland—it was our community, our block. I always knew that I had a homeland; and now, when people ask me where my home is, I say, "Montgomery, Alabama."

But the northern kids didn't understand that they had a homeland.

They had to make great efforts to connect with each other. They had come from so many different communities that they didn't have the sense of homelife and homeland.

GRUNBERG: So you didn't feel that marginalized status Baldwin wrote of?

DUKES: I remember all the qualities of second-class citizenship that I felt, but Montgomery was my home. My surroundings were so connected that it didn't bother me. I knew that I could not go to Oak Park to swim, but it didn't bother me. My tub in the backyard was where I could dangle my feet. I felt very comfortable.

GRUNBERG: Did your private home and community life override any other feelings you might have had?

DUKES: Absolutely. It gave me a great sense of pride and confidence, because every house on my block was my home. We ate at each other's houses. We clothed each other. We shared. We romped and played all day long.

GIAMO: But you say that this is not the situation today for the inner-city younger generation?

DUKES: Absolutely not. They are an "endangered species."

GRUNBERG: To many people today, it seems that Nelson Mandela might be an answer to some of this. If he can get into power and help to run a better South Africa, this will have a positive psychological influence among blacks here in America.

DUKES: While I do not think that role models are the cure for all this, they can have a powerful effect. I work with the Coalition of One Hundred Black Women, and recently we were involved in a program called Project Lead. We went up to a center in Harlem where the Girl Scouts had recruited a group of young black girls. We were given the opportunity to talk with them, and we talked about ourselves first. The coalition consisted of investment bankers, lawyers, advocates, and other professionals. Some of the parents attending had never been around black women who were professionals. Their eyes started opening up.

We won those children over and, I suppose, they won us over, because we were only supposed to make one or two visits but we decided to get more involved. There were only fifteen of them, but I believe that we helped to save these kids from becoming mothers at the age of 12 and 15. And that's because they felt better after our visits. We may have helped to save a generation, because they felt good and now they will tell others and exert peer pressure.

We had the police come up and show them all the drug paraphernalia. Then we asked the children what they would do if they saw somebody with this stuff and they said that they would run and tell their teachers and report it to the police. We got their minds all psyched up.

GIAMO: Yet the media relay many more negative role models, don't they?

DUKES: They don't get paid to tell success stories.

GRUNBERG: Who are some of the role models that you look up to?

DUKES: I look up to Dorothy Height, who is the president of the National Council of Negro Women. She is about 75 years old. She took over for that organization after Mary McLeod Bethune. I also look up to Gwendolyn Baker. I met her when she came to New York to work at the Bank Street School. We had African American parents working as teachers aides and, after that experience, many of them went on to college themselves. This was a very important program. It got parents involved with the education their children were getting. Their children would see this and it would encourage them and their whole family.

GIAMO: It has been said by some critics that one of the causes of homelessness is racism.

DUKES: Well, you know, when I walk through Grand Central Terminal, or Penn Station, I never take a count but I see whites too.

GRUNBERG: I think this comes from the fact that blacks, and other racial and ethnic minorities, are overrepresented among the homeless. In the New York City shelter system, for example, 70 to 80 percent of the homeless "residents" there are black.

DUKES: But whites are there too, and there are more older white people than black who are homeless.

GRUNBERG: It is common, however, to hear advocates, especially black advocates, complain of racism as one of the ultimate causes of homelessness.

DUKES: Well, there are certain areas around this nation, and in New York state, that will not allow affordable housing in their communities. These are "exclusive" communities, and your only choice, if you don't have a lot of money, is to take to the forests. But then where is the employment around there going to be?

In another sense, there are people who are not being given an adequate education. So if you look at a lack of quality education or of equal opportunities, you end up getting pushed around by a lack of choices, especially if you don't have many skills or if you've been a manual laborer (which is now a virtually nonexistent occupation). So, yes, racism does become part of the broader issue. It is not the total part, but it can perpetuate the social ills that we have. If a person cannot read or write and lives in an impoverished area, something has to give in order for that individual to get out. There is just no doubt about it.

GRUNBERG: And if something is not given, then you are going to go nowhere. That is where the racism comes in.

DUKES: That is exactly where it comes in.

GRUNBERG: On the way over to your office this morning, I bumped into a former homeless man who is now an advocate for the homeless. Upon hearing that I would be talking with you, he suggested that I ask you the following question: what do you think of the idea that there is a white conspiracy against black Americans? Is there, in effect, a conspiracy of silence? In the face of so much systemic suffering, do we need to talk about the possibility of such a conspiracy?

DUKES: There is a conspiracy of silence. Just yesterday, I heard Reverend Forbes' sermon and I couldn't say it any better. His message was essentially this: "Let my leaders go." He said that he hated to disrupt anyone's summer vacation but that, as you go ahead and plan for your vacations, you ought to be thinking about the need for leaders to come forward. He also talked about homelessness. He said that right across the street there was both a dangerous and, at the same time, an endangered species of black males. So, yes, I would have to say that there is a conspiracy of silence, but it exists among black leaders as well. No one is sitting down and making an urgent call to do something about all of this. That is the silent part.

GRUNBERG: What I am now trying to do in midtown Manhattan is tell the business leaders that, if they don't involve themselves beyond volunteerism (though that is a good start) to providing the necessary linkage to entry-level jobs, then there will be no lasting solution. The homeless will remain on the streets until then. This seems to be a message they respond to, however slowly.

DUKES: You have to do that. They [business leaders] don't sleep here. They go back to Connecticut and their staff members have to do all the complaining. Their workers have to travel the subways, and the subways stink. Okay, so you have to get these business leaders to respond, but that process too suggests a conspiracy of silence.

GRUNBERG: Currently, in one of the programs I am running we are making an effort to bring together two groups of people—the business community and the homeless. Each group typecasts the other and there was an opportunity to bring them together, to get to know each other better. They play basketball against each other. They sit in workshops. They take meals together. We are developing a mentor program so that some of these relationships can continue. Entry-level jobs are opening up for the homeless. All this and more simply from the social process that has opened up since these two groups have begun to relate.

DUKES: You have to get people mingled. You have to get people mingled so that they understand that they are all human beings. They can give each other basic respect and basic dignity. Once you do that, people respond differently and they behave differently. But you need leadership for this to happen.

GRUNBERG: You are really talking about attitudes, aren't you? The passivity of leadership, of even the homeless themselves?

DUKES: Absolutely, yes.

GRUNBERG: What changes attitudes? What can be done?

DUKES: Little things as you've shown—programs that work. When I went to Harlem, none of those children or parents had ever seen black women who demonstrated such success or who carried themselves this or that way. All they've seen is the police busting the dope dealers. And the media feed into all of this. But, you see, now they encounter black women. And you know what is so phenomenal about Jesse Jackson is that he said, "I was adopted. I was a bastard child. On Thanksgiving Day we were waiting for my mother to bring turkey bones while we played basketball." Young children sit in amazement when Jesse starts talking. The same thing with Mandela. People stood in line to meet him. Sometimes there were 5,000 people in line.

GRUNBERG: Waiting for inspiration?

DUKES: They were waiting for inspiration. "You can do it. They did not break your spirit. They kept you in jail for twenty-six years. You came out tall, standing straight, not even bent over." His footsteps may have been a little slower, but his mind was sharp. I was there when he took Ted Koppel on. They showed people in South Africa saying bad things. Mandela responded, "I am not washing my dirty laundry out." So that gave people a sense of confidence. They begin to think: "All this stuff they're throwing at me, I can handle whatever comes my way. If I've got something in my mind that I want to do, I can do it."

GRUNBERG: Is there a role for affirmative action in the pursuit of social justice and equality?

DUKES: I don't think that we can even pursue justice and equality on the basis of affirmative action. I don't think so. I think that you have to proceed from the economics of business. And the federal government has to come up with a massive program for the inner cities. And there has to be a welfare reform bill where people are not denied whatever they work for. If you work and make $400 in a month, welfare will only give you $100. I mean, where are you going to live? Where are you going to eat? It's better for you not to work and get your $600 all from one place.

There is a young woman who works for me and one day she had to run and talk to Long Island Lighting Company about the installment program in which she didn't have to pay her whole electric bill at one time. They asked her to sit and wait until she was called. She left here on her lunch break and, before I knew it, she had come back to work and asked me if she could go the next day and try again. You see, if you have a job, what are you going to do? LILCO closes down before you get out of work. They are not open on Saturday or at night. What are you going to do? Eventually, you're going to give up, stay home, collect your $600, and pay the light bill. You are knocked out on every side. You have to be extremely strong just to keep some dignity.

GRUNBERG: Along the same lines, there ought to be day care programs in the inner city?

DUKES: Exactly. All they have to do is change the school hours and keep them open longer. If the mother wants to have a job and she works until five o'clock, and if she takes the subway, she won't be home until six o'clock.

GRUNBERG: I suppose if we can get Menachem Begin and Anwar Sadat to sit together, we can get leaders—black and white—to come together and emerge with a plan.

DUKES: Absolutely. Why do we have a secretary of Health, Education and Welfare? We need those people to sit down there first and talk about all the money we are spending just on their department's issues. For example, please believe me, I am against smoking. But why are they all sitting there, spending all that time and money on this one issue when they could be accomplishing other things? There are other actions they could initiate to help make people healthy. You are healthy when you feel good about yourself, when you have a job and some dignity.

GRUNBERG: It seems that in the 1950s and 1960s there was some sort of path that we were on.

DUKES: Yes, we were.

GRUNBERG: Each year things got gradually better. What stopped that?

DUKES: Reagan stopped that. And now we will see what Bush will do.

GRUNBERG: But the people around the country voted both of them in, repeatedly.

DUKES: But you couldn't find anybody who voted for them after the election. Once again, there's the silent conspiracy at work. Now the test is going to be who Bush really is.

GIAMO: When King was leading the Civil Rights Movement with Andy Young, Julian Bond, and others from the Southern Christian Leadership Conference and its affiliated groups, the issues were very direct and clear-cut. They were fighting against certain fundamental injustices and looking to attain civil and political rights. The problem then was very concrete—segregation.

DUKES: But it still is now—when we get enough people who will say it. The constitution of these United States does not spell out, if you will, quality education, decent housing, employment opportunities. But it does say liberty and justice for all. You read liberty, then you define liberty, and you see what you come up with.

GRUNBERG: And the pursuit of happiness?

DUKES: You cannot be happy if you cannot pursue quality education. You cannot pursue happiness if you don't have a job. Happiness? Nobody gives you happiness. You work for happiness, and then it comes.

GIAMO: I suppose the difficulty here is that African Americans are moving to another level of equality—both conceptually and practically beyond the conditions of integration. It involves the realization of social and economic justice.

DUKES: Social and economic justice has to be a part of it. It was that way with King. The economics of the situation were there.

GIAMO: But once basic civil rights and political equalities are granted, once you win that battle and start striving toward greater social and economic justice, what happens?

DUKES: You can win the battle but still be losing the war. If I don't have a job, sure I can buy a hotdog. Sure I can go to the Sheraton Center and sleep. Nobody is going to turn me away. They will only turn me away if I don't have a credit card—if I can't pay for the room in advance. So that is the pursuit of happiness. But that battle was won. You then have to give me the *opportunity* to be able to make the money to afford these things.

GIAMO: Those opportunities are still not there.

DUKES: Absolutely not. If I can't find employment, I am still not going to be able to go to the Sheraton Center—not until I can get the money.

GRUNBERG: So the door is open, but you still can't get into the room.

DUKES: All of the issues related to equality and justice have not been solved because of the silent conspiracy. Racism is real.

GIAMO: And it is not so easy to point to anymore because the concrete situation has been removed, at least in the courtroom if not in actual practice. Blacks can ride at the front of the bus, they can eat at the

83

counter, attend certain schools via the provision of school busing, and they can go wherever they wish.

DUKES: If they have the money.

GIAMO: But the question of money (and economic injustice) is often concealed, isn't it? I'm trying to get at the difference between overt oppression (the obvious forms of segregation) and a very distanced and hidden—but nonetheless powerful—form of oppression.

DUKES: It's not hidden. It's not hidden. The silent majority knows it.

GIAMO: Is this yet another example of the silent conspiracy?

DUKES: Well, the conspiracy is there. A white person can have a third grade education and go into a place where racism is found and still become employed. A black with a college degree will have four or five interviews and will still not be employed.

GIAMO: Once again, access to vital and well-paying jobs is still blocked.

DUKES: Absolutely.

GIAMO: And that retards the movement toward greater social and economic justice.

GRUNBERG: So we should not kid ourselves that the problem isn't clear. It is, and that is why there is talk of conspiracy.

GIAMO: But is it "visible" to the social eye?

DUKES: Of course it is. Why do you think people fought affirmative action?

GRUNBERG: What about the tolerance level? We say that the outlook is bleak because of attitude and the fact that the only hope seems to be for unlikely political action. At what point will people say, "Enough! Enough of this long wait for political action. I have waited long enough. I'm going to take to the streets"? Do you think that could happen again? Or has society become too splintered and complacent for this sort of response?

DUKES: No, no. That kind of response is very possible. That could happen again. It could go any day now. I never think that it can't happen. I wouldn't be surprised.

When you find all the people, such as yourselves and the advocacy groups all over the nation, trying to do all that you can, you're bound to see that the tolerance is wearing thin and the level of frustration increasing. Sadly, the people you are trying to help do wear out. After all, they are human beings, and just as you or I become frustrated, they too must do their best to keep on tolerating the situation day after day. In the end, they can go either way.

GRUNBERG: Isn't that something voter registration is supposed to be tapping? Isn't it supposed to ensure that people do not fall silent?

DUKES: For most of them, I don't think that their anger would become a silence. I think that their anger would most likely become an explosion.

GIAMO: On the national level, what is needed to overcome the problems of homelessness and poverty in America? Can you provide some perspective and offer several priorities?

DUKES: When I was a kid we had the WPA—the Works Progress Administration. It was part of the New Deal. Now, my grandmother told this story; she was a great storyteller. When Roosevelt died, my grandmother sat on the front porch and cried. I was very young and I didn't understand, so I asked her why she was crying. I knew that nobody on our block had died. She said, "My best friend died today." She had heard it on the radio. "Who is your best friend?" I asked her. "President Franklin Delano Roosevelt," she said. "How did he become your friend?" I asked. "You've never been to Washington." She looked right at me and said, "When you give everybody a job and some food, then you become a friend. And he did it with respect and dignity."

And, you know, as I got older and started studying sociology and psychology, I learned that anytime you want to give people dignity you do it through work. And even if you don't make much money, and you have to get on line for food, at least everyone in that line is on the same level. Nobody is degraded. Nobody feels stigmatized.

So I'm saying that somebody in the federal government needs to come up with a vision which will give people dignity. There are a lot of people out there who are poor, but they still have a sense of pride. They aren't proud of being poor, but nonetheless they do have pride. All homeless people are not dirty. I've seen women at Penn Station in the bathrooms washing out their clothes. They don't want to smell. They are going to wash their clothing. So this should tell you that there needs to be a vision which gets people to tap into that underlying strength and pride. And it has to be job-related. Whatever you give to them, also give them a way to pay you back.

First of all, we must come together with a vision at the federal level. That is why I talked about the New Deal. We have to sit down and come up with something. We have lost manufacturing jobs, which were jobs for African Americans and for new immigrants, such as the Hispanic and Asian communities. Second, there must be a foundation of support. When you have a job there has to be affordable housing out there. And there need to be accepting communities out there, because—though you need to have a job—you also need support systems to go along with that job.

So the priority has to be the realization of a shared vision that will bring people together to form supportive communities. And these communities should be planned to maximize support. There have to be grocery stores not six or seven blocks away from your home, but nearby. That is what you call a community. Community consists of having those conveniences that you and I have. I live on 68th Street, between Second and Third avenues. There are five grocery stores in my immediate neighborhood. I take my choice. There are four cleaners. I take my choice.

GIAMO: That is a very different concept from what some coalition advocates insist is needed. First, you are saying that we must secure good employment opportunities; and, second, it is not simply housing, but constructing homes within viable communities that we must accomplish.

DUKES: It is both employment opportunity and community that are needed. Self-esteem should also be considered. It is an extremely important personal and social quality to attend to. People have to feel good about themselves. Again, here is where the community plays a major role. Its activities have to be uplifting, whether that means good counseling services or a school where people can safely mingle, and which is open in the evenings.

GRUNBERG: A sense of increasing confidence in both self and community must be developed.

DUKES: Absolutely. There is no other way.

JAMES R. DUMPSON

The Social Welfare

BENEDICT GIAMO: In retrospect, it seems that the 1960s were very similar to the 1930s in setting new public policy initiatives to address poverty and inequality in American society. As we move further away from the 1960s, into the 1970s, 1980s, and 1990s, what is your assessment of all the initiatives and programs that we call the War on Poverty? Where are we now?

JAMES R. DUMPSON: I'm not one of those people who disowns or minimizes the contributions of the War on Poverty to the social development of the United States. As you know, there are people who say that the War on Poverty was a dismal failure, that we squandered all the money in programs that didn't do anything, etc., etc. Not so in my judgment. Social change in the United States has always followed a constantly incremental process. In social policies and changes we are not a revolutionary people; we don't have revolutions that turn the system over. The War on Poverty, and its related programs, comprised just one more important phase in the incremental social development of public policy in the United States. The social welfare programs that we have in place now and based on my concept of incremental social policy development (measures such as entitlements and the right to income when employment is not available or possible) evolved as a result of the War on Poverty and its many experiences. You know, we talk about work experience, the right to work, and we have training programs in the welfare department, and we have public assistance, and we talk about the level of public assistance being inadequate. All of this came out of the experiences that this country had to go through in order to develop a certain standard of social and economic justice for its people.

JEFFREY GRUNBERG: During the inception of the War on Poverty you were the commissioner of social welfare under Mayor Wagner in New York City. What was the national scope of poverty at this time? How did the nation define and approach the social problem?

DUMPSON: The concept and definition of poverty had by then become useful as a tool for defining government's role in describing national policy and in moving the country to acceptance of the imperative to reduce if not eliminate poverty. Remember at this time [1963] there was a woman in the Social Security Agency, Mollie Orshansky, who statistically defined poverty for the very first time in the United States. The poverty levels as they are known come out of her research on minimum food requirements related to level of nutrition. By the way, she never intended to define poverty. She was making another point altogether, but then the bureaucrats used her work and institutionalized poverty to mean a level of economic income required to maintain various levels of living. So it was also at this time that we began to talk about poverty in terms of housing, health, and education. These were four major social issues around which the federal government and Health, Education and Welfare, in particular, really began to move.

GIAMO: Who then among the American people needed the housing, the health care, the education, and other essential human services?

DUMPSON: Then it was the poor, yes, just the poor: those who statistically had income to purchase a minimum level of clearly defined goods and services. Now, we knew then that when we said the poor we were talking, to a large extent, about blacks. And it wasn't until later in the wars against poverty that we began to say, "Hey, they aren't the only people who are poor." We found Appalachia, we "discovered" Appalachia at that time. Of course Appalachia had been there all along, that whole cultural region from southwestern New York right straight down through southwestern Pennsylvania and into West Virginia. Here were the poorest of the poor, worse than most black communities even in the South. So then we began to talk about the poor other than blacks. We began to talk about poverty in the Mexican American communities of the Southwest. We began to talk about the Okies. We began then to discover patches of poverty in our urban centers, really groups of people all living below the poverty line and who had lost their ability and will to move and were no longer associated with the American dream. And they were described as shiftless and irresponsible; we blamed the victims of social and economic deprivation. They became regarded as the undeserving poor.

Incidentally, it was about this time [1965] that the full implementation of the tenets of the dream of the Social Security Act of 1934—insofar as health was concerned—became implemented. As you know, Medicaid and Medicare didn't come along with the New Deal public assistance programs of the 1930s and 1940s. It is reported that Roosevelt made a compromise during 1934 and 1935, when the Social Security Act was up for acceptance by the American people, and then later by the Supreme Court. Roosevelt knew that he would not get health; it was omitted as the price he paid to get income assistance as an entitlement package. I think it was always a dream of his that he would come back one day to health care and "nationalize" that system just as he had "nationalized" the income support system. But, of course, he never did. So it was not until years later that any rational health component in the social security system was enacted, and, in accord with social policy development, we are now groping toward some form of health care as a national entitlement.

GIAMO: What were the major problems facing New York City at the time you were commissioner of social welfare (1959–1965), and how did these problems compare with those faced by other cities around the country?

DUMPSON: First of all, the problems in New York City were no different than the problems of Chicago, Los Angeles, Houston, Atlanta, Boston, and the like, except in numbers. At the root of the problems to which you refer is poverty; poverty is a national phenomenon—it is not peculiar to any one city. For every manifestation of poverty, we had it ten times more than anyplace else. So there was nothing about social problems in Los Angeles or Chicago or Atlanta or any other major cities that distinguished them from New York City, except size and numbers. And the national disgrace is the failure or inability of our political leadership to recognize and accept this fact.

When I was commissioner under Mayor Wagner we finally counted a million people on public assistance. But we had something in the Wagner administration that those cities did not have. We had a mayor who had come out of a very liberal background. Robert F. Wagner, Jr., was the son of Robert F. Wagner, Sr., who had written most of the labor laws in Congress. It was his father who had crafted most of the labor laws in the United States Congress.

By the time Robert F. Wagner, Jr., became the mayor of the city of

New York, we had a very liberal mayor who believed government to be one of the primary instruments for helping people—not the agent of last resort. It was, therefore, relatively easy for me as both social worker and commissioner to get support from Bob Wagner to use his leadership to command policies and resources of the city government for doing something about poverty. I remember that he was Catholic and I was Catholic and yet we had here in New York City the first family planning program in public welfare in the country.

GIAMO: How did you bring that off?

DUMPSON: I said to the mayor, "Look, we've got mothers and their children in growing numbers on AFDC and very soon the public assistance rolls will be unmanageable. But, more important than that, these women are raising children, bringing children into the world who do not have a fair chance and the young mothers are not aware of a choice." And he said, "Well, what are you getting at?" And I told him that I thought maybe women were having babies because they didn't have an educated choice with access to family planning services and to reproductive counseling. And he said, "Have you talked to the cardinal of the archdiocese about this?" We were talking politically then, and I said, "No." He said, "Well, I think you ought to go up and talk to Monsignor Guilfoyle," who in those days was the head of the Catholic Charities of the archdiocese. So I went up to see him and he gave me a long lecture about church doctrine until I interrupted him. I said, "Monsignor, I'm not here as a parishioner; I'm here as an executive talking to an executive." And though I put it politely, I did say, "I'll get my religious instruction in my parish, but I'm here to talk to you as a public official, one executive to another, responsible for provision of services that people in need have the right to select once they know the facts—the right to know and to choose." And he said, "Well, if you do what you say you're going to do, we will publicly criticize and oppose a program that makes available family planning services in the public agency."

And I went back and told the mayor, and he said, "What do you believe people need and what do you believe is right to do?" I told him that I wanted to change the policy and offer family planning counseling services to people on public assistance as a matter of choice. I assured him that I would instruct my staff and that the services would not be forced on anyone. He said, "If this is your best professional judgment, and if you think it's the thing to do, then go ahead and do it; but remember that you're going to be severely criticized and I won't be able to help you very much. Nevertheless, you do what you think has to be done in the interest of children and families receiving help from your agency."

So we changed the policy, and as quick as we did the newspapers had a field day. To my knowledge, we were the first public welfare department in this country to offer women referral to family planning services. Of course, we had to make some compromises. Women had to be over 18 years of age and we could only offer family planning as one of a number of services. Further, we didn't offer it ourselves, but we would refer them to family planning services outside of the department. Although we couldn't offer it ourselves, the policy was that these women had a right to know of the service and to be referred to the service if they wanted it. Similarly, we felt we had an obligation to refer families or individuals to whatever services they needed. And about two or three months later the state of New York mandated this as a policy for all of its public welfare departments in New York state.

GIAMO: At that time homelessness was really confined to the Bowery of New York, and to other skid rows around the country, as it had been since the late nineteenth century. Did you have any policy initiatives to work with the homeless on the Bowery?

DUMPSON: Yes, there was an organization that's still in existence called the Manhattan Bowery Corporation. We had shelters for homeless men, and remember we're talking about homeless men—that was the population at the time.

GRUNBERG: Was the term—"homelessness"—used then?

DUMPSON: Yes, we talked about homeless men, but not in the same way we talk about homelessness today. We're talking about a group of men on the Bowery with an average age in the mid-50s, many of whom were alcoholics, and 90 percent of whom were white. And we would pay

the flophouses (they were lined along the Bowery) a dollar or a dollar
and a half a night to shelter these homeless men.

GIAMO: As one man I met on the Bowery during the late 1970s put it:
"I'm a bundle of paradoxes." In fact, isn't it paradoxical that the homeless men who were on the Bowery, or on other skid rows throughout the
country, found their "homes" in these institutionalized settings for the
disenfranchised?

DUMPSON: That's right.

GIAMO: If we define homelessness strictly in literal terms, then they
weren't the "truly" homeless that we have today. Most, if not all, of these
men did have a roof over their heads at night, and at least skid row did
mark off an urban territory, a neighborhood if you will, for the down-
and-out. But that's about all.

DUMPSON: That's right. We had not discovered homeless families at
the time. In fact, I think if you had asked us about them in those days we
would have said, "Oh, they're here and there." We did have some families
who were dispossessed for nonpayment of rent. Although we did have a
shelter for women—for single homeless women—but it only held twenty
or thirty women in it.

GIAMO: Down on the Lower East Side of Manhattan, on Lafayette
Street?

DUMPSON: Yes. We didn't have shelters for families because we took
the children to foster care. We, the city and my department, operated a
temporary children's center in the building known as Children's Center
on Fifth Avenue at 104th Street. It had many good programs but it was
still congregate care. Sometimes we would have two children sleeping in
a bed because of the overcrowding. While its purpose as a temporary
facility was usually forfeited, we didn't have large numbers of homeless
families sheltered together as we have them now.

And I remember doing a study during my tenure under Mayor Wagner
and found the numbers of children I had under care who could have

returned home if we had had housing for them. And I publicized that fact because it underscored the finding that a basic underlying cause of homelessness was the absence of low-cost, affordable housing.

GIAMO: And what year was this?

DUMPSON: That was around 1960, 1961, 1962.

GIAMO: That was a prescient discovery. I know that one objective of the Manhattan Bowery Corporation, which also emerged in other cities, such as Chicago and Philadelphia, was to scope out the skid row areas for urban renewal opportunities, while at the same time doing objective and quantitative studies to get information on the characteristics of skid row and the men who lived there. I recall that there were some plans during the 1960s for urban renewal on the Bowery, and in other skid row areas, but they were never developed, and yet, throughout the 1970s and 1980s, we have seen a great deal of urban renewal and gentrification in and around New York City which is, perhaps in part, a fulfillment of that original objective in a very different form.

DUMPSON: Talking about urban development, let me just say that one of the contributing causes of homelessness and homeless families in the 1960s was urban development. We displaced families. By gosh, look at Lincoln Center and the numbers of families that were bulldozed out of areas in the name of urban development. That whole area—Lincoln Center for the Performing Arts, the opera house, Fordham University—was, to a certain extent, an early contributing factor that paved the way for the emergence and growth of homeless families. What did we do? We built Lincoln Center, but if you remember there was a housing development just in back of Lincoln Center, right there on Amsterdam Avenue. Well, that didn't even begin to house the numbers of people who had been displaced. So urban development in many instances almost became synonymous with displacement of families. We had not learned the interdependence of social and economic planning. We try to help other nations accept this interdependence as a cardinal principle of national development, but we resist institutionalizing it in our own policy development and programs.

GIAMO: If you don't look closely at it, the problems of homelessness throughout the 1980s, and now into the 1990s, seem to have appeared out of nowhere. Yet, as we've been talking here, it's obvious that there has been a developmental process.

DUMPSON: Yes.

GIAMO: What then has caused homelessness to grow so rapidly throughout the 1980s? It is now regarded as one of the leading social problems of our times.

DUMPSON: Well, I think there are a couple of factors that caused this. One was the displacement that came about from urban development. For all of the pluses that we can give to urban development, we must remember that it also contributed to homelessness. It didn't leave people necessarily out on the streets, but it did begin the process of overcrowding and doubling up. Families had to move because they were tearing this down and tearing that down either for a new apartment house that went up—way out of range price-wise for those displaced people—or for an office building, factory, cultural center, etc.

GRUNBERG: So the sense of community was being shattered.

DUMPSON: Oh, it disappeared. Who talked about a sense of community? They were interested in development. So this was one very subtle but I think frequently unrecognized contribution to the development of homelessness that we have with us in the 1980s and 1990s.

The second was our inability to keep up with the rising increase in poverty. I don't think that anyone can look at the homeless situation without recognizing that a major contributing factor is poverty—the absence of income to purchase housing. And I don't mean to purchase housing through ownership, but to pay an affordable rent for it. The gap between the numbers of people who needed housing and the small supply of affordable housing out there—affordable in terms of income, available income—became more and more of a problem over the years. And, as your poverty rates went up, that gap became wider and wider. So that was the second one of those incremental factors leading to the rise of homelessness.

A third one, of course, was deinstitutionalization. Back in the mid-1950s we got the bright idea in mental health policy that we were going to close (and there were good reasons for doing so) the large state mental hospitals throughout the country. And we were going to develop psychiatric centers at the community level that would be supportive of the psychiatric needs of the people who were deinstitutionalized. Well, we did deinstitutionalize, but we never put the other pieces in place. We never set up those community-based psychiatric support services.

So you have the adverse effects of urban renewal, poverty, and the absence of affordable housing, and added to that you have a large number of people who cannot live without psychiatric support, and the supports aren't there. And, finally, we witnessed in the Reagan years, and now the Bush years, the abandonment of any federal responsibility for low-cost, affordable housing.

G R U N B E R G: We spoke to Herb Pardes about the mental health aspects of homelessness and he was quick to point out that, at the time this social policy was being debated, psychiatrists themselves were divided. Many didn't think it was a good idea, many did. And Richard Lamb, who recently wrote a piece on deinstitutionalization, blamed the naivete of psychiatrists for their inability to get funding they thought would be there, and for their failure to anticipate and understand the extent to which NIMBY [not in my backyard] would reoccur to frustrate community mental health efforts. It's kind of surprising to think that there could be such naivete. Was it naivete?

D U M P S O N: I don't call it naivete. We don't have the political will to deal with NIMBY today. Just this afternoon the mayor of the City of New York [David Dinkins] talked to a group of us about a health center that needed to be relocated. And the commissioner of health said he was having some problems in finding a location. In fact, he had word from some council members that they didn't want this health center where he was planning to put it. The mayor said that he would like to follow through with the original plan, since the commissioner told him that it was the best place for that health center. The mayor then went on to say,

"I want to tell those council members that we're going to put it there unless they come up with some alternatives that satisfy our criteria. We'll be unpopular, but we aren't going to let NIMBY determine the public policy of this administration."

GRUNBERG: So the failure of deinstitutionalization had a lot to do with political will, or the lack of it?

DUMPSON: Of course, of course. And it had to do with the public perception of mentally ill people. They were regarded almost like the undeserving poor in the poverty categories. They're seen as outcasts and we're threatened by them.

GRUNBERG: Was deinstitutionalization then, in part, a statement that the government was making on poverty?

DUMPSON: No, it wasn't. As a policy, deinstitutionalization was devised on the basis of humanitarian impulses. Supported by the latest of scientific advances, they really wanted to do something for those who were mentally ill but who really did not need state mental health care. Now, it was also going to be less expensive. It was going to be cheaper to have people living at home in their own communities, and it was going to be socially more desirable.

Then, of course, we never increased income entitlements of the public welfare to keep up with the cost of housing until we had families. Anna Dehavenon has done a lot of studies on the relationship between the level of public assistance and the increase in homelessness. We had this large population of people who counted on public assistance. We increased the housing allotment very slowly, if at all, and so the people more and more who were dependent upon public assistance couldn't pay the rent. So they were dispossessed, and where did they go? Out into the streets and then they got into the shelters. As rent and poverty rates escalated, the income level of public assistance remained static. So then, eventually, this evolved into a whole new major contribution to homelessness.

GRUNBERG: So, ironically, psychiatrists are getting a second chance. Many of the mentally ill are being reinstitutionalized in shelters and warehoused in large buildings around the country. Now there's something that has to be done again.

DUMPSON: But you can't keep people who are psychiatrically disabled in large group settings. So they aren't getting their chances. Psychiatrists ought to be out there fighting the shelter mentality as a means of caring for people who are homeless.

GIAMO: Do you feel that the problems of homelessness, as you have outlined them, are adequately understood by the public, the media, government officials, and advocates?

DUMPSON: No, no, no, no. For most people, homelessness reflects a group of shiftless, irresponsible individuals and families who refuse to pick themselves up by their bootstraps. People never think of breaking it down into this group must be dealt with this way, this group must be dealt with that way, this group must be dealt with in still another manner altogether. Homelessness—they just say, well, homeless families . . .

GRUNBERG: "They all need a home."

DUMPSON: Yes, "They all need a home." And I regret to tell you that there are large numbers of the homeless who, if you gave them a home, a house tomorrow morning, would be back in the shelter six months from now unless you've dealt with some of the precipitating problems that created their homelessness. And part of that is their inability to adjust socially and to have the economic support from gainful employment or by an adequate income entitlement that assures acceptable patterns of living.

GRUNBERG: As well as their inability to develop social networks?

DUMPSON: Yes, social networks, but then we take them out of the shelters now and we put them in apartments up in the Bronx and we leave them. You not only need housing, but you need the supports to go along with the housing. Now, you know, they'll relocate a mother and three of her children from one of those shelters and put that family up in the Bronx, and nobody will say anything about where to find schools, health facilities, counseling services, and day care centers so she can go out and find work. Nobody connects them with a social support system—supports that every individual and every family needs in order to make it today.

G R U N B E R G: It's almost the undeserving poor syndrome all over again. "Just cast them out."

D U M P S O N: "Get them away, get them out of sight." So the homeless situation needs a variety of initiatives.

G R U N B E R G: It seems somewhat bleak. We were talking to Hazel Dukes about the notion of a conspiracy. Not that people are sitting in a room and saying, "Let's see how we can keep the poor poor"; but there does appear to be a conspiracy of silence. It seems that many of the leaders know this to some degree and are just not doing anything about it.

D U M P S O N: Well, you know, that's true, but it's true for another reason. It isn't that they're closing their eyes. You know as well as I do that 85 percent of homeless families are people of color. When you think of that fact, and when you say that people just don't want to face facts, it isn't that they don't want to face facts—they don't want to face a lot of facts that have to do with people who are different. There are policymakers and politicians whose racism or racist impulses keep them from even acknowledging what has to be done, because so many of the homeless are black or Hispanic or have been discharged from jail or a mental hospital. They are second- and third-class citizens.

G R U N B E R G: In any case, they are "undeserving."

D U M P S O N: They're regarded as undeserving.

G I A M O: So the solution to the social problem of homelessness, those three initiatives championed by the coalition advocates and mass society—"housing, housing, and housing"—is in fact another way to mystify people from attacking the real nature of the problem. And it seems to me that this is a very insidious form of conspiracy (if we're talking conspiracy) because it has to do with cultural perceptions affecting how we see the problem, how we name it, and how we fight against it in such a way that blinds us to other pertinent questions concerning race, class, gender, poverty, power, and social control.

DUMPSON: Exactly. Exactly.

GRUNBERG: Well, that leads right into this question: in a 1987 Human Services Task Force Report of which you were chairman, *Falling Behind: A Shelter Is Not a Home*, prepared at the request of then borough president David N. Dinkins, the group stated that, although blacks comprise only 14 percent of New York state's total population, nearly 60 percent of the homeless across the state are black, again reflecting the role of poverty in homelessness and underscoring the extent of poverty in the black community.

DUMPSON: Yes.

GRUNBERG: And yet committees are formed, reports and books are put out, and facts are presented in a very public way. But this kind of disproportionate figure persists despite all this activity, the public record, and the awareness that comes out of it? Why?

DUMPSON: You know, if you looked at the major social problems that we face in our country, you can't name one to me that doesn't have as a contributor the reality of racism. And, of course, by racism I refer to racial and color differences, which I think is more rampant in the United States than economics and class differences. But I define racism not as antiblack or anti-Latino; rather, I define it as a mindset that defines certain people as inherently inferior. And, you see, with this definition we could have racism of people who are white as well. This happens in American culture.

GRUNBERG: "White trash"?

DUMPSON: Yes, "white trash." But the definition includes all people

who are seen as inherently inferior. And once you say "inherently inferior," you have signed, sealed, and delivered their fate. And there's nothing that the state or religion or anybody can do if such people are regarded as inherently inferior.

GRUNBERG: Even the efforts embodied in affirmative action?

DUMPSON: If you accept my definition, affirmative action is not a response to racism. And that raises the question: how do we bring about
change in the mentality that is demonstrated through racism? How do
you modify behavior that has racist attitudes as its motivating force? I
don't know the answer to that. And let me tell you, with all the advances
made by the Civil Rights Movement it really has not cracked that nut. If
so, you wouldn't have people tolerating Jesse Helms in North Carolina.
Actually, he has a good chance of being reelected to the Senate despite
the fact that he's the archracist in that state [Helms was reelected to the
Senate in November 1990].

GIAMO: So race is another contributing factor to homelessness.

DUMPSON: Yes, it's race as well.

GIAMO: Racist perceptions and policies.

DUMPSON: Yes, yes.

GIAMO: What about the economics of poverty and homelessness? We
are told that money is tight right now and, in fact, there seems to be a
fiscal blockade against any new initiatives in addressing poverty issues
and the problems of the homeless. Often, the problems and policies of
the 1980s are cited as justification for this blockade: the "trickle down"
theory of supply side economics, income tax restructuring, deregulation,
increased military expenditures, the federal budget and trade deficits, and
the saving and loan bail out.

DUMPSON: Well, money is tight, but we're also just stingy as a nation.
Nobody can tell me that if we wanted to we couldn't right all the things

that have gone wrong and that have been depressing large portions of the population into poverty. So I just have to say, parenthetically, that we are stingy. I don't know any other way of putting it. Just look at this current business of ours—the "read my lips" attitude. Hell can cover us over with debts: "Just read my lips; there will be no taxes." Why? The mentality is this: "I don't give a damn about all of this, and I'm not going to pay for it."

G I A M O: Is this neglect a form of stinginess or does it represent a cultural strategy to regulate the poor? That is, the nation gives the poor enough in transfer payments and in-kind benefits not to pull people out of poverty but, at best, to maintain their social condition. On the national level, does this practice reflect incompetency or intentionality?

D U M P S O N: Intentionality.

G I A M O: Is that a conscious strategy?

D U M P S O N: Yes, in part, but I think it depends on whom you're talking about. I think you have to individualize that. I think there are some people for whom that is intentional—either they just don't care or it's tied up with their racist feelings. And their racism may not be necessarily just against blacks or Latinos; it could also be divided along the deserving and undeserving poor continuum.

G I A M O: Perhaps regulating the poor also works to justify the American middle-class ethos and the dominant cultural values of individualism, competitive struggle, and upward mobility.

D U M P S O N: That's right. "If I made it, you can make it." One of the worst things I hear, something that really annoys me, is when people say, "Well, you know, the immigrants who came to this country in the late 1800s, they made it. Why can't Latinos and blacks make it now?" Well, the social and economic environment is not 1890; it's 1990. What, we've got a service economy now; we've got a faltering school system.

G I A M O: You talked earlier about the growing disparity between income and the cost of housing for the poor, and it might be helpful to mention, in passing, that the movement from a manufacturing to a service-oriented economy generally depresses wages. Also, from 1977 to 1984, New York City alone lost 95,000 manufacturing jobs.

DUMPSON: Exactly, and we never put those two things together.

GIAMO: Why don't we ever put things together like that? Why do we keep mystifying the problems?

DUMPSON: Well, if you use your intelligence and put them together, you also become very uncomfortable.

GIAMO: With the implications?

DUMPSON: Yes, with the implications. So you protect yourself by mystifying the problems and you become very comfortable with that.

GRUNBERG: Maintain the status quo at any cost.

DUMPSON: That's right. You get very comfortable with that.

GRUNBERG: Let's move into solutions. Do you think that the roles of task forces are taken seriously?

DUMPSON: I think that task forces are very important to the process of managing a city. Sometimes we're lucky, sometimes we're not. The last time we were very lucky. We had a borough president [David Dinkins] who listened to task forces and used them as a means to educate himself. And we were lucky that he later became mayor of the city. He sat today and talked about things that came out of different task forces that he had sponsored. There is no question in my mind that many of his outlooks on homelessness come out of *A Shelter Is Not a Home* [a task force investigation and report Dumpson co-directed on homelessness commissioned by David Dinkins as borough president of Manhattan]. Where would he have gotten those insights if we didn't have a task force? And where would he get the legitimacy for his thinking if he didn't have it backed up by the work of a task force? So education and credibility are vital to the purposes of task forces.

Second, task forces give professionals and their colleagues a sense of participating in policy development and this fulfills the designs of participatory democracy in government.

GRUNBERG: So are you pleased with the impact of *A Shelter Is Not a Home*?

DUMPSON: Oh, yes. Whom did the mayor select for his office of homelessness? Nancy Wackstein. Where was Nancy Wackstein? She was one of the two people who staffed the task force on homeless families. The other person was Marcia Smith, who directed the research and on whose findings the task force developed its recommendations.

GIAMO: What are some of the recommendations from *A Shelter Is Not a Home* that you expect to be implemented by the current administration?

DUMPSON: Closing all the shelters. That's the basic one. Another recommendation that has been implemented (not sufficiently, but it's underway) is the rent allowance in the public assistance program. Shortly after the report came out, the state increased the rent allowance—not sufficiently—but there has been a move upward of the rental allowance to the poor. We also recommended not closing the cases on welfare recipients for strictly administrative reasons. Once this was implemented the number of families who had had prior public assistance experience going into the shelters for homelessness decreased. It didn't decrease the total population of homelessness, but it did decrease the incidence of homelessness for those who had a prior public assistance status.

GIAMO: When you say close the shelters down, does that mean you're going to be moving the homeless families into more permanent housing arrangements?

DUMPSON: Even the Koch administration had a deadline for the removal of all families out of welfare hotels. Now the Dinkins administration is saying that we will always need shelters for homeless families in a city this size, but those shelters are going to be quite different from the shelters that are now in existence. We're now talking about individual family units in a congregate setting as well as multiservice and small reception centers. I hope the Dinkins administration will move to the Swedish plans of transitional housing, which involve the social preparation of families. Since so many economically and socially deprived families have had to move so often from substandard housing, one must keep in mind that their inability to use adequate housing only gets reinforced.

G I A M O : What about the huge shelters around the city for single men? Some of them, like the Fort Washington Armory, bed down anywhere from 800 to 1,000 men per night. Will those shelters be maintained or is the current administration planning to phase them out as well?

D U M P S O N : No. Keep in mind that these policies immediately call attention to the fact that we have a hierarchy in groups among the homeless: families, then women with children, then children, and, lastly, homeless men. Those men will probably stay in those shelters.

G I A M O : Or perhaps be back on the Bowery.

D U M P S O N : Yes, or back on the Bowery. We're talking again about the deserving and undeserving poor. This is our heritage.

G I A M O : I'd like to take us from the local to the national level. It seems that since Watergate there has been a growing skepticism, and even contempt, for government. In fact, there are many Americans who seemed to have lost faith in the idea that we can develop public solutions to deal effectively with some of the nation's most pressing problems. In your opinion, do you feel that there is, at present, a crisis of confidence in American leadership and governmental action?

D U M P S O N : Yes, there is, and for the wrong reason I'm afraid; that is, our expectation of government is higher than our expectations of any other form of production or of providing services. Let me give you an example. Yesterday, the New York City commissioner of health, William Meyers, found that in previous city administrations all of the results of pap testing had never been fully reported and, as a result, there are women walking around whose pap examinations or tests are positive. His position was that the Department of Health had lost credibility as a result of this. You know, that's a strong statement. But if General Motors has to recall 5,000 cars, we haven't lost faith in GM. We have one standard for government activity and performance and we have another standard for the private sector.

G I A M O: What are the national policy initiatives you would recommend to President Bush today in regard to poverty and homelessness?

D U M P S O N: First of all, I would recommend any number of policies that would be aimed toward reducing poverty in this country to an absolute minimum, with its elimination a national goal. That would be number one. Second, I would have the federal government go back into the housing business and do what the federal government can do best, that is, to create housing that is affordable to low-income families. About ten to fifteen years ago, the federal government went out of the housing business. So from a policy stance, I would say to Mr. Bush go back quickly into building affordable housing and community support structures (schools, stores, hospitals, etc.) across this country. And then, of course, we've already talked about other initiatives: service provisions, stabilizing families, and preventing the breakdown of families who are victims of poverty and urban renewal.

But I would want to be careful of the service aspect of policy initiatives because I believe that if you give people enough opportunities, money, and education, then we won't need "all these services" that my profession talks about. Service might become residual for the people who are left out of the system, but I don't want to see us build up a social service economy that says people must be dependent upon somebody helping them. Social and economic conditions should support people to be self-directing—to have enough money, jobs (and, if people don't have jobs, then somebody's got to give them money), and the opportunity to use that money to purchase goods and services, which includes housing. Then 90 percent of Americans would be self-directed and might need services only when something catastrophic happens in one's life, but not as a bulwark against the use of one's will, one's sense of self-direction, one's opportunity to achieve self-realization, self-fulfillment.

GIAMO: What about private initiatives? It seems to me that if we want to fit people into the restructuring of the economy, and prevent poverty and homelessness, then we need a stronger partnership between the private and public sectors.

DUMPSON: Absolutely.

GIAMO: Do you see this happening?

DUMPSON: Well, of course, government at the moment—whether in the present administration or the one that preceded it—does not view itself as a partner. When you talk about partners I think of equality. Mr. Bush doesn't see that. Mr. Reagan, perhaps a better example, certainly didn't see it either. Both of them want (or wanted) government out of everything. There's no partnership concept in that posture. Just leave it to the marketplace and the benefits will trickle down and everyone will be fine. That's their position. But if you want to talk about public-private partnership, then it seems to me that we're talking about equal responsibilities and the provision of opportunities from both sides for individual and community development. I hope we learn from this and from the mistakes we've made in the past.

HERBERT PARDES

The Politics of Mental Health

JEFFREY GRUNBERG: Given all the social problems in this country, do you think that psychiatry is referred to often enough by other professions, or the general public for that matter, for definitions, solutions, or policy decisions?

HERBERT PARDES: Yes, I believe there has been considerable improvement. I think that psychiatry has been experiencing a renaissance in the past ten years or so. The respect for it has grown as its treatment impact has increased; there are more treatments, they are better, and they help a lot of people. If you look around, I think you will see that there are people who are psychiatrists now in prominent positions not necessarily calling for a psychiatrist, which I think is an interesting sign. The head of the Carnegie Foundation, the president of Duke, and the Medical School deans at Emory and South Carolina are just some of the psychiatrists that come to mind who are not in traditional psychiatric positions.

As for psychiatry as a field? Yes, Congress asks psychiatry for its opinion on everything under the sun. We get calls constantly from the newspapers and the broadcast media. The thing to be careful about in this regard is that psychiatrists, when they speak, should speak authoritatively without going beyond their knowledge base. That is the one thing that concerns me about these trends.

BENEDICT GIAMO: How do you think the media have fared in communicating the social problem of homelessness to the general public?

PARDES: There has been a fair attention to the problem of homelessness, but not as much as I think there should be. I think that the media try to bring disturbing social issues to the country's attention. The problem lies with policymakers today who say they are interested in these problems, but don't do anything substantial about them. We have a president who says we have major problems with highways, with drugs, but I don't see the resources going forth to do anything about these things. Pragmatism in political strategy says it is dangerous to suggest raising tax revenues because then you can be booted out of office. Do you see a major program in housing? I hope that [Jack] Kemp will be able to do something despite the political context, but I do not see it yet.

GRUNBERG: In some parts of New York City, and elsewhere around the country, the business community is hiring professionals to help home-less people who are living on the streets in the vicinity of their shops. Insofar as businesspeople command many resources, and as time passes and government does not act, perhaps we will be increasingly turning toward them for the enhancement of existing services to the homeless.

PARDES: I think that it's encouraging if businesspeople feel that way, but the basic problem will not be corrected unless the government real-izes that we have created a situation that restricts available housing for people who are indigent. They have no place to go. If you could give these people some secure financial support and make sure there is enough low-income housing around, then there will be a place for them.

GIAMO: This leads into an obvious question: who are the homeless and what should we be doing for them?

PARDES: I think that the first thing you have to do is realize that they are not a homogeneous population. So what you should be doing for them depends upon what produced their homeless situation.

GRUNBERG: What do you do if you cannot find the right kind of "home" to solve a particular person's problem?

PARDES: If it were up to me, I would try to figure out the array of things that cause homelessness. Then I would try to respond with services that attend to that array of issues. So, for example, if there is a family that cannot afford its apartment, then that is a financial issue.

GRUNBERG: Nationally, what has been or what should be the role of psychiatry?

PARDES: Currently, psychiatrists should advocate a new national policy. National policy depends on local responses to what has been cov-ered by federal programs in the past. Now, it is true that some good people will step forward and do all sorts of good things to help some homeless people, but that does not take the place of national policy, which would be aimed at all homeless people. We have had a national policy of obliviousness.

GRUNBERG: How the public comes to understand a social problem, or how the politician comes to respond, is tied together with how a problem comes to be stated. Advocates are often the ones who first call attention to a problem. But they will often state a problem in the simplest of terms. In the case of homelessness, some will say, "Rehabilitate buildings, not people. Don't try to change the subject to mental illness, or drug abuse, or even poverty. There are only three things to talk about: housing, housing, and housing." Doesn't this undermine the sort of comprehensive approach that you are talking about? Or do you believe that advocates succeed if, at the very least, they get people to begin problem-solving processes?

PARDES: I think that advocates try to draw attention to something. They can be simplistic. But still what they are trying to do is speak for the person who cannot speak up for himself or herself. That does not mean the response need be simplistic or that you have to do what they say. But you should look and see if what they are trying to get you to pay attention to is worthwhile.

GRUNBERG: It appears sometimes as if the general public looks to the psychiatrist as the knight in shining armor. "Put them back in the hospital. You released them. Rescue us all from your earlier mistakes." Do you think that the public overestimates the role of psychiatry as a profession that can provide ultimate solutions?

PARDES: Psychiatrists are not experts in housing or in financial matters. And it was not psychiatry alone that was responsible for deinstitutionalization. Often it was policymakers concerned about the budget who thought it was a good way to save money. They set goals for state hospital directors, such as reducing patient populations to 90 percent, or 80 percent, or 70 percent, whether or not the patients were ready to leave.

GRUNBERG: Sociologists such as Erving Goffman, writers such as Ken

Kesey, and other figures comprising the popular culture of the times championed liberation as a theme during the 1960s and 1970s. As a profession, did psychiatry join in with those members of society who called for freedom? In other words, did psychiatry lead the way or did it merely respond to economic imperatives?

PARDES: Like any other profession, psychiatry is not monolithic. So there were psychiatrists who said that there was an excess of hospitalization and others who said that some people will do better if you give them a chance outside the hospital. Basically, there were three big problems. One, community resources were not delivered to meet the need of those discharged. Two, there was a switch in the laws, which I think swung a little too far in the direction of sensitivity to the individual rights of the patient. In doing that, lawyers made it extremely difficult getting a person into a hospital. This problem is what is referred to in the phrase "dying with your rights on." And three, the economic exploitation of what was basically a good idea (for some but not all patients) from the vantage point of better psychiatric care. These points indicate that it was not psychiatry alone that contributed to the failures of deinstitutionalization. Actually, there were many psychiatrists who argued vehemently against it.

GRUNBERG: Dr. Richard Lamb spoke out, saying that, basically, the homeless mentally ill were victims of naivete. He said, and I paraphrase from an issue of Reaching Out, a newsletter which speaks out on issues regarding mental illness, that there were simplistic notions of what would become of those discharged. The importance of psychoactive medication and a stable source of financial support were perceived as necessary, but the importance of developing fundamental resources and supportive living arrangements were often not clearly seen. Community treatment had been discussed but there was little formulation as to its structure. The NIMBY [not in my backyard] syndrome was not anticipated. Isn't it difficult to accept that psychiatry could be so naive about these very important and seemingly obvious things?

PARDES: Psychiatrists were not unanimous in favor of discharging many of the patients, but they were not immune to the pressures of economic imperatives usually set by others. There were a lot of people in on that. Let me give you an example of how an imbalance has been created between patients' needs and their rights. When I was out at Colorado State Hospital a case came to the court for assessment as to whether or not a particular patient should be in the hospital. The lawyer for the advocacy group was very strongly for discharge of the patient. There was a court dispute between herself and the psychiatrist. And she won on some technicality, so the patient was released. In a fit of enthusiasm, the lawyer said to the patient, "If you want, I will give you a ride back to the city." Then she grew somewhat frightened by the patient's acceptance of her offer. She went to the psychiatrist, whom she had just defeated, and asked for advice as to what she should do in case there were any problems along the way. The psychiatrist said that if the patient got agitated, she should ask him to get out of the car. Tell him to take a walk. During the drive the patient did become agitated. The lawyer followed the advice of the psychiatrist and stopped the car, allowing the patient to leave. The patient went to a nearby clinic, attacked a social worker, and went right back into the hospital. So what was accomplished?

GRUNBERG: And the lawyer went to the psychiatrist she had just defeated for advice. Apparently, she believed that the psychiatrist possessed knowledge that would help her go beyond the patient's needs in favor of her own.

PARDES: Let me give you another example from a series of articles that appeared recently in the papers. A young schizophrenic male gets released from a state hospital. He goes home and beats up his parents. The parents are terrified and they ask the authorities to put him back in the hospital. The authorities talk to the man, who reports that he is feeling fine. They conclude that they cannot put him back in. So now the parents are living with this kid who may attack them at any moment.

GIAMO: Is it the prevailing opinion among psychiatrists today that deinstitutionalization has gone too far?

PARDES: Yes! If you ask most psychiatrists, they would say that it is too difficult to get patients to the hospital. People are so concerned about protecting patients' rights that they are making it difficult to treat patients. Actually, it is a close call. The opposing view would be that patients' rights were not attended to sufficiently in past years. Perhaps now it could be argued that we have overswung the other way.

GIAMO: I was reading E. Fuller Torrey's book *Nowhere to Go: The Tragic Odyssey of the Homeless Mentally Ill*, in which he criticizes the policy of deinstitutionalization. He says that, first of all, not only did fewer community mental health centers appear than promised (although 2,000 were planned nationwide there ended up being less than 800 in existence) but, second, these centers strayed from their original mission. They were supposed to be treating the seriously mentally ill, but they became more preoccupied with mental health and, as Torrey puts it, with the plight of the "worried well." He cites this as an indictment against psychiatry and community organizers.

PARDES: Well, it is always easy to blame somebody. I think that there were many people who had a determining influence on the way community mental health centers were set up. But community mental health centers had a somewhat ambiguous mission. As you say, they were originally supposed to take care of the most seriously mentally ill. On the other hand, also important was work based on the realization that, through early case findings, you could, in some instances, prevent some problems or exacerbation of problems. However, we must realize that people with very serious illnesses are not easy to treat. But it is not only psychiatry alone that tries to help and either does or does not succeed. I am sure that, in some cases, the staff of some of the community mental health centers tended to work with those people they thought they could help; perhaps those people were less seriously ill. Additionally, there were many people who worked at these community mental health centers who cajoled the state into discharging nearly every patient. These staff members were not just psychiatrists; they represented all the mental health disciplines, and often the board and administrative staff members.

Now, the Community Mental Health Center program was interrupted. I was running the National Institute of Mental Health when this happened. The goal was 1,500 centers and we stopped at about 800. But it was not stopped because it was failing. Many of us were working to make the system more responsive to the seriously mentally ill. What stopped the program was a change in the presidency. While the Carter administration was interested in mental health services, the Reagan administration said, "Send the money to the states and let them decide how to spend it. They'll take care of it." So the federal government walked away from a responsibility to mental health services.

GIAMO: And what did the states end up doing?

PARDES: Fifty different things. And one of the problems, for example, is that Mississippi and Massachusetts are not the same, so you do not have a homogeneous program. One of the things that federal support accomplishes is some kind of consistency. Additionally, you can get systemic and extensive programs on the federal level.

So we said to the Office of Management and Budget, "Don't you want to evaluate the effects of turning the Community Mental Health Center programs over to the states?" They weren't interested in what the effect of the policy change would be. They did not want to have any responsibility for it. The federal government was, at that point, espousing a policy which the people in this country voted Reagan in on—that the federal government was involved in too many things and that it should get out and let the localities take care of them.

We had also been working very closely with Housing and Urban Development at the same time to develop more housing options for the chronically mentally ill. That disappeared. Now maybe this has been somewhat resuscitated, and the Robert Wood Johnson Foundation is putting some nice things together, but a lot of time and a lot of good programs were lost.

GRUNBERG: In some quarters, the emphasis is still on down-sizing government. But what is being stressed here is that the federal government needs to provide the leadership as well as the structure.

PARDES: Absolutely.

GIAMO: It reminds me of a remark made by the late President Kennedy. He said that about 6 percent of Americans are rich enough to hire lobbyists to protect their interests in Congress but, he asked, "Who is looking after the other 94 percent of Americans?" And he pointed to himself in answering his own question, "The president of the United States, that's who."

P A R D E S : Joe Califano used to conceptualize the federal government's Department of Human Services as the nation's conscience, as representing the nation's compassion. I was at the National Institute of Mental Health during the years 1978 to 1984. Jimmy Carter was there until 1981. In those three years we worked on the Mental Health Systems Act. We worked very hard to craft it and, finally, to get it passed. And then, within seven months of Reagan assuming office, the act was essentially scuttled. The act made provisions for special programs for minorities, children, the elderly, and the chronically mentally ill. It was trying to direct itself toward some of the things that community mental health centers were not doing. We had also put together, during those three pre-Reagan years, a big plan for the chronically mentally ill. But this too was all but scuttled.

G R U N B E R G : During the "Billie Boggs" case here in New York City, I remember being struck by the fact that the lawyers, who were defending her right to refuse the prescribed treatment, had proven that "Billie Boggs" was capable of making social connections with people outside of her peer group. That is, they developed a relationship with their client that, unfortunately, the psychiatrists could not develop.

When working with psychiatric patients who are homeless, I have found that their resistance is perhaps their eleventh hour attempt at self-help. That is, if you accept their so-called resistance as reasonable, and you work toward developing a relationship with them above all else, then you usually end up with patients who will want to become involved in treatment. They may not accept all that you want them to, but you will get a foot in the door and, eventually, they will accept more and more. Most people, homeless or not, do want what is best for themselves.

P A R D E S : Often, it is hard to resist getting into an adversarial situation. That is what our current system offers and sometimes demands. What is the fight all about anyway? The focus should be on what does this patient, this person, feel. Why are they out there? How are they hurting? How can we help them?

GIAMO: Additionally, it seems that there is a battle of ideology that has been shaped by the very nature of all the different disciplines. It is not hard to imagine where the differences among and between psychiatrists, social workers, and psychologists, for example, might lead.

PARDES: I think it is very healthy of us, however, to be working so hard at protecting people's rights.

GIAMO: What about when we are protecting the constitutional right of certain people's life, liberty, and pursuit of happiness by keeping them on the street? Don't you think that this is a perversion of our intent to uphold their rights?

PARDES: Yet I have not heard of one conceivable reason why, in this particular day and age, a psychiatrist would want to keep someone in a hospital who does not want to be there. They are not going to make any money out of it. Doctors do not want to see people suffer.

GIAMO: But it seems as though psychiatrists often end up responding more and more to human rights issues in the abstract, legal questions, political fears, and economic incentives than to the existential realities that appear in our nation's cities.

PARDES: Perhaps in one sense, however, we are discussing the exceptions. I think that, in the overwhelming proportion of situations, there is going to be little disagreement among people about what is best for the patient.

GRUNBERG: Many of today's homeless are institutionalized and many of those improperly discharged have actually been reinstitutionalized. Scattered as they may be in shelters, drop-in centers, churches, SROs, terminals, known urban "campsites," and in jails or prisons, most of these mentally ill homeless people [some 250,000 nationwide] are known by social service and outreach programs, emergency room and soup kitchen staff, the police, and welfare workers. In this sense, they have been regathered. Again, however uncomfortable or distrusting, they are accessible. Do you see this as presenting psychiatry, for example, with a second chance?

PARDES: If I was in city or state government, and I had governmental policy responsibility, I would create a task force and bring together the five or six major disciplines. This would include housing, finance, psychiatry, law, and general health care. I would say that we have one, two, five, or 10,000 homeless people in our community, and we need to develop a prescription to help each individual.

GRUNBERG: You would develop pathways of improvement for each person?

PARDES: "Pathways" is a good way to think about it. You would ask regarding each person, "Which pathway would best fit you?" And you would get input from the various disciplines and see how you could make it work for him or her. I would also say that there are areas of the country where there are jobs available. There should be a government-sponsored skills-training and reemployment effort for all those homeless who would work but who are unemployed.

GIAMO: You would try to reconstitute a WPA-like program?

PARDES: Exactly. What will you do for people, almost immediately, if you help them regain employment? You will restore their confidence and self-esteem. If they feel they can do something useful, the changes can be dramatic.

GIAMO: I am interested in what seems to be a concern of yours—that you view the solutions for the problems of the homeless in the context of local community. Is there a question of critical mass here? If the services encompass too large a geographic area, do matters get too complex?

PARDES: I could handle this on a national level. You just have to decide on your conceptual approach. And the concept may be that you organize around the role of the case manager. Taking part in a support program, for example, each case manager could have a caseload of twenty-five or so. Each would be part of a team of representatives from the various disciplines. Now you have a system that stresses connectedness.

GRUNBERG: If you could do that, in the end, you still would have some people who would show little improvement.

PARDES: There are some people who are so dysfunctional that they might be better off in some kind of institutional setting.

GRUNBERG: And the staffs of these institutions would make sure that a patient's stay, however long it may need to be, would be as short as possible. And the discharge plan would involve one of these pathways.

PARDES: Absolutely.

GIAMO: And the resources should come from local, state, and federal government agencies?

PARDES: That's exactly right.

GRUNBERG: And you might want to get business resources in there as well; they have the jobs and, in the right set of circumstances, they have the will as well.

PARDES: Business could help around the edges, but this is a *government* problem.

GIAMO: In a situation like we have now, where there is no cohesive national policy with funding and resources, what happens to hospitals? Insofar as they come into contact with homeless people, what kinds of institutionalized stress do hospitals experience, if any?

PARDES: You can extend that further and more concretely. Hospitals feel that they are being asked to take on the care for people for whom they have no money. Hospitals try to stick to the operating principle whereby they do not want to turn patients away. However, if government won't pay for people who cannot pay, then you are going to have a lot of hospitals in financial distress.

One of the unfortunate tendencies of our political system is that politicians spend much of their time trying to get reelected. Their goals become political and short-term, rather than geared toward solving these long-term problems. And I do not mean to trivialize these problems, because they are very costly and very complicated. But we should have insurance coverage for every single person in this country. Then, if a person walks into a hospital, he or she will not be treated as a second-class citizen.

GRUNBERG: In a discussion I once had with a psychiatry resident who had a special interest in the development of psychiatric treatment, he offered the following thought: with the advent of medication, psychiatrists slowly have lost their creativity. That is, prior to medication, they had to be more creative with their patients; in order to successfully treat individuals, they had to pay more attention to family structure, to the quality of the patient's support system, and, most importantly, to the patient's own perspective. Do you believe that there is some truth to this—that inventiveness has receded somewhat?

PARDES: That is possible. There are probably some who rely on medication too much. I am a great believer that psychiatrists should know about medication and about psycho-social treatments and should try to give the patient what fits the patient.

The psychiatrist who simply prescribes medication and does not pay attention to the patient is not doing good work. Incidentally, it is often nonpsychiatric physicians who give the medication and they don't do as well as psychiatrists in the accuracy of their prescriptions. They don't know as much about such medication and they are not as likely to pay attention to the patient as an individual.

GIAMO: How did you get involved in the profession of psychiatry?

PARDES: I was interested in health care early on. In college I became intrigued by courses in abnormal psychology. I wanted to know what made people tick. When I went into medical school, my choice was between internal medicine and psychiatry. And although I liked internal medicine and admired people who were very astute diagnosticians—who could figure out complicated situations—I found out that outpatient medicine was much more psychiatric in tone than inpatient medicine because there were so many psychological, psychiatric, and social problems in the actual delivery. I opted for psychiatry, which I felt would involve less repetition.

GRUNBERG: It almost sounds as if what could not be repeated in a laboratory was what you found attractive about psychiatry.

PARDES: Absolutely. The notion of being a person who would do the same exact procedure the rest of my professional life was not attractive.

GRUNBERG: Where do you feel the strengths and weaknesses lie in the training of psychiatrists?

PARDES: I think that the training of psychiatrists is becoming more comprehensive. There is much more attention to training in psychobiological matters and pharmacology. Of course, you have to be careful that a program does not swing too far that way. I think that some programs could pay more attention to rehabilitative strategy. But psychiatry programs are going through changes; some have paid too much attention to psychological matters at the expense of biology.

GIAMO: Do you feel there is a place for the humanities in the education and training of psychiatrists?

PARDES: Yes! I think that psychiatrists generally are very responsive to the humanities. Psychiatrists as a whole are interested in a wide range of issues and disciplines. The wider their interests, the greater the likelihood they will connect psychologically with their patients.

GIAMO: Do you have any overall policy recommendations for addressing homelessness, not just for the mentally ill homeless, but for homeless people in general?

PARDES: The most important point from my perspective is that homelessness has to be dealt with as a heterogeneous group of situations. Second, the services should fit the person's needs and rights as an individual. Third, we should integrate the various services and then use them according to what the person actually needs. So I would recognize differences and treat them accordingly. I would like to see treatment that acknowledges that homeless people have needs, hurts, desires, and wishes just like other people. They are just not one of a multiple. As far as policy goes, we also have to educate the American people about the fact that we are dealing with human beings who are in trouble, not just a depersonalized group.

I would like to say one last thing that I feel very strongly about. There is a philosophy that characterizes this country and I think dignifies it as well. It is one which says that this country is only as good as the way it treats its most needy citizens. No matter how difficult or problematic these citizens may be, if we don't take care of them, then we have failed.

Part 3

The Shapes of Social Conflict

ROBERT JAY LIFTON

Victims and Survivors

JEFFREY GRUNBERG: For over thirty years you have been concerned with the inhumane conditions and human consequences of victimization and suffering, especially in relationship to the Holocaust and Hiroshima. Do you believe that suffering is relative, and, if so, where do you see the homeless along the continuum of suffering? Or is suffering absolute?

ROBERT JAY LIFTON: No, suffering is relative. There are different degrees of suffering. But it all hurts; it's all painful, and the homeless seem to me very far along the scale of suffering. I was thinking, in anticipating this dialogue today, that most of the people I've studied have been victimized by a specific event: the Nazi camps, Hiroshima survivors, even people affected by the Chinese thought reform movement; or victims of smaller disasters, relatively smaller, such as Three Mile Island or Buffalo Creek. When I and others studied these victims, we would find ourselves pained by the exposure to them. I remember when studying Buffalo Creek we would be very relieved at leaving that area of West Virginia when we finished our particular visit, because it was so painful to spend even a day or two in and among a community of people who were undergoing grief and pain.

Anyhow, the homeless seem to me to be sort of perpetual victims now, rather than the consequence of a particular event of victimization. They have quickly become perpetual victims. They're here in our city and in other cities and without that entity that couldn't be more primal—a home. And for most of them it's perpetual in that there is so little relief. I know there are programs that help but it must feel perpetual for most of the homeless. So, to answer your first question, there is something very primal about their suffering and you could compare it in various ways with the suffering of Hiroshima survivors and death camp survivors, though I hardly care to. They are victims and survivors. But they're even deprived for the most part of the one source of vitality you covet in that setting—some meaning structure in relation to the survival that can enable survivors I've worked with, or some of them, to reconstitute themselves, get back on their feet, find significance in their survival, and even make constructive use of it—a survivor mission. There are some among the homeless who do that. But one has the feeling that there are precious few of them, and that most are in the grip of despair. So they lack some of the survivor attributes or sources of revitalization.

I'm struck very immediately by how the homeless draw us into their plight, because they're here, they're around, and many people say in different ways that we can't avoid them. Even the Hiroshima survivors and the survivors of Nazi genocide could be avoided to some extent. They're out there. But you could call forth some numbing, as I call it, and it wouldn't take much to go on with your life and not be much aware of them. Of course, we do that with the homeless, but we have to look at them. They thrust their homelessness right before us and they ask us for money or for some attention—at least a number of them do—and they're instrumental for making life in New York City more unpleasant. When people talk about why the quality of life in New York City has become worse, radically worse in the last few years, I think it has much to do with the homeless and beggars. (They're not exactly synonymous, but they're close as anything else.) What that means essentially is that it becomes much harder to numb yourself to the plight of people who are hurting in New York. There've always been many of them, but they've been out of sight. They aren't now. Therefore, it's painful for people with any sensitivity at all to simply walk about and live in New York. And I speak personally here because I share in their pain. To carry that further in relation to the kinds of work I've done, it really means that all of us have to cope with more numbing, more dissociation, in order to live in an everyday way in New York City. And that's a very profound matter because it really means we have to become increasingly dissociated as human beings, as a society, as people who live in American cities and who like to live in the cities.

In my last book, *The Genocidal Mentality: Nazi Holocaust and Nuclear Threat*, I talk in some detail about the dimensions of dissociation in relationship to Nazi doctors on the one hand and Western nuclear weapons designers and strategists on the other. Though very different, they share certain characteristics and central to those characteristics is dissociation at various levels. In the case of both of those groups there is doubling at the center, that is, Nazi doctors had to double in order to perform a separate functional self, the Auschwitz self as I call it, or the Auschwitz doctor. Doubling also existed among the nuclear weapons designers and strategists, but not quite to the degree of Nazi doctors because they weren't killing on a daily basis, or they wouldn't see the results of killing right around them. Nonetheless, it was a form of doubling. And the point I made is that there's doubling at the center and numbing at the periphery, so that most of the German population had undergone considerable numbing and there was a parallel process with the American population in relation to nuclear weapons. We see it again reactivating itself in connection with the Persian Gulf—easy talk of war, but with protective devices to avoid imagining accurately what would really go on at the other end of the weapons: horrible killing, suffering, tens or hundreds of thousands, maybe millions of people dead, if they were exposed. Instead one calls forth various ideological plans, as has been true for the Nazis or the nuclear weapons situation, as a way of blocking off that moral imagination. One calls for patterns of dissociation that are mediated by ideologies.

Now, with the homeless we do undergo forms of dissociation—all of us—in order to live in New York City and other cities. It doesn't completely work, that is, it doesn't prevent us from guilt, shame, pain, and conflict. Should you stop and give them money? I'm sure that the kinds of experiences I've had—walking together or coming from a film with my wife—many, many New Yorkers have had. Typically my wife says, "Look, we've got to help this man, this woman. She's sitting there with a baby." And I say, being the male abstractor, "Well, what's the use, you know. We're not going to solve anything by giving them a dollar or ten dollars. Let's just go on." And we argue between us: should we stop or go on? Sometimes we stop; sometimes we go on. It's not satisfactory in either case. There's no satisfactory resolution. So translating that struggle between us, or that conversation, should we call forth more dissociation or should we be immediately humane to a person who is clearly suffering? While recognizing that it's not going to solve his or her problem, but might be a decent act and, in a way, runs the risk of us opening up further our own guilt and shame and problems by the very act of stopping and taking in that pain.

BENEDICT GIAMO: It's interesting how it works on us because it is so immediate; it is so visible.

L I F T O N : Yes, palpable; we experience it and that's crucial. There are different ways of saying that. I'm saying it in terms of my work or what I've learned from other studies, but some version of that visibility, of that palpable involvement, occurs on the part of everybody along with the pain that such encounters cause us. I'm sure this will come up in all these interviews because it's somehow at the heart of our relationship to the homeless problem.

In my way of looking at it, I place great stress in all of my work on the problem of dissociation in the form of numbing, or now doubling. I thought of writing a book called *The Age of Numbing* to say something about what happens at our moment in history and, whether I write this book or not, it's a central issue for me in our time. And it's a way of talking about this call to numbing that is made to us all the time which most of society falls in with. It's a way of talking about what's wrong with us and with society; for instance, the nuclearists or the leaders of our society, as with Bush right now and others promoting war. The call to numbing can also be a call to war; this can be simultaneous. Or a call to nuclear stockpiling. And, above all, this spoken or unspoken dimension of the message is "Don't feel, don't feel the pain you're going to inflict and experience. Shut it out and listen to my ideological call." And then there is the whole process of narrow, insipid nationalism and war-making.

Also, my work with Vietnam veterans is parallel in a different way. It is also a call to numbing that they went through. I felt with some pain the experience of insight and something valuable in working with them, but they spent years trying to undo that numbing in the process they called "becoming human again." So the kind of dissociation that we're called upon to make in regard to Nazi victims, nuclear weapons today, war-making, and homelessness is dehumanizing. It diminishes us as human beings in the most significant, primal ways. It harms us as much as it harms them.

G I A M O : In that sense, can you regard the members of society as being in some way victimized as well as being less than human?

L I F T O N : Yes, we are victimized in some real way. It doesn't mean that we want to hold to that image of ourselves exclusively as just victims in this whole thing. But we are victimized in the sense that we're thrust into a broad social problem which our leaders and our social machinery are resistive to and do little or nothing about (or what is done is inadequate). And we're made to feel the pain in insoluble ways. So in some sense we share pain that's for us insoluble.

But, having said that, I wouldn't rest on it. It reminds me of the whole issue that I discussed with people in Hiroshima not too long ago, maybe six or seven years ago in the early 1980s. It was what they called victim consciousness. Many people have spoken of it in different ways with a specific Japanese term for it, what they call *higaisha-ishiki*, which really literally means victim consciousness. And these were intellectuals in Hiroshima thinking about Hiroshima as a city and A-bomb victims or survivors and where they were at that time. And the problem of course with victim consciousness is locking yourself into an identity of the victim and, in a way, immobilizing yourself in terms of action against a real evil.

GIAMO: In a way, it sounds like academia. Intellectuals in academia tend to identify with many marginalized groups, and in going through the process of articulating the concerns of these groups it seems like that expends all of their energy. Political inactivity often results.

LIFTON: Academia has lots of other problems, including, centrally, moral problems. But, yes, I think if an academic rather accurately lays out what's really wrong with society, even boldly, and then is completely immobilized—does nothing—then there is a blanket in front of anything in the way of real action, or even social commitment, or let's say public expression—some sort of public activity in combating that evil. That failure or inaction is likely to be accompanied by some sense of, "Well, I'm a victim of this as well, therefore, I'm helpless before it"; or "I'm helpless before it, I'm a victim," whatever order one says that in. So, yes, I suppose it is pretty close to being parallel.

GRUNBERG: If you didn't experience some numbing you wouldn't get home or get your work done.

LIFTON: Well, that's right. When I think of numbing it's a kind of long continuum and part of it is the numbing of everyday life, some of which is necessary to all of us. Both of you have described working with the homeless. That means that you've opened yourself to their pain more than 99.9 percent of Americans or anyone else has. Nonetheless, you too have to numb yourselves or call forth some degree of numbing in order to go home and have some enjoyment in your lives and then even write about the homeless.

The best way to start in trying to grasp this kind of issue is to start with oneself. Before I did my Hiroshima study and conducted the actual interviews, I had done a lot of thinking about Hiroshima, talked to people openly—they told me a good deal about it and I learned a lot that had to do with the study and about the experience of people in Hiroshima. I could manage that all right—talking about the problem. Then I initiated the detailed interviews. The very great detail in their descriptions of exactly what they experienced was powerful—physical experiences, the levels of fear, the imagery, the anxiety, what they saw. They described everything to me. They fully opened the whole tale to me. Those first few days I heard those things I was overwhelmed. I felt anxious; I couldn't sleep well at night. It happened that I was alone. My wife and young child hadn't moved yet from Kyoto where we had been living before, and I was alone at an inn doing these first interviews. I began to think, "It's impossible for me to do this study. I know it's important and it should be done, but maybe I'm not the one to do it. It's too painful." But within a matter of days those feelings greatly diminished and I felt calmer. I began to focus on what people were telling me and what it meant psychologically. In other words, I developed what I came to call "selective professional numbing." It was necessary for me to do that in order to do the study.

But, of course, it's a kind of warning about how we can readily numb ourselves professionally and, of course, I never stopped feeling some of the pain, but felt less of it. I struggled for some balance really. This is what we do as professionals when we deal with any really painful subject. Usually, we go too far in the numbing and don't allow enough of the pain in. But it is some balancing act at best when we're dealing with really painful subjects as you both have and as I have, and that is a real lesson. And, of course, the path in which I came to that terminology was that in interviewing survivors I noticed one of the first things they told me about in great detail was how they experienced the bomb, saw these horrible scenes around them, and suddenly felt nothing. And they just saw these people walking around aimlessly whose skin was macerated, dripping and bleeding. The most unbelievable scenes and suddenly they felt nothing. We talked about that and that's how I came to what I first called psychic closing-off. And, although it was absolutely different in degree and dimension from what I was describing in myself, I came to a conviction that there's a continuum. In the most extreme forms of exposure to pain and threat there's the numbing of the victim or survivor that I could observe or hear about in talking to Hiroshima survivors. But there's the numbing of everyday life at the other end of the continuum and the numbing of those who study painful experiences also at the relatively milder end of the continuum in terms of emotional experience, but pretty painful to those of us who have been through it.

GIAMO: You've written that "the profoundest insight is attainable only by the survivor: he who has touched death in some bodily or psychic way and has himself remained alive" [Robert Jay Lifton and Eric Olson, *Living and Dying* (1974)]. Considering the person who is suffering, and those who are responding to this suffering, what is the nature and power of such insight?

LIFTON: The nature of that insight has something to do really with a grasp of some truth about death and suffering one hadn't had before. It's more direct with the person who has been through it—the survivor—but I think some of it can be conveyed to the student or the investigator. One way of getting into that subject is through this experience that I've had. Very soon after I came back from Hiroshima, in 1962, I began to pull together some of my findings and to talk to different groups, including antinuclear groups and psychiatric groups, such as Physicians for Social Responsibility. And I noticed that when I spoke before psychiatric audiences I would give my talk and it would be very intense, because I would convey some of the horrors that had been conveyed to me. And the audiences would be silent for a moment afterward. They would respond very intensely in various ways when asking questions. And then there would be other speakers. And a few people told me that they deeply resented other speakers speaking after me, because something was happening to them when I spoke that was then interrupted when other speakers came and simply talked about ordinary psychiatric issues. And I understood what they meant. It's as if one was taken into a realm of pain and death that ordinarily one doesn't have access to.

Another example that comes to mind is the first trip that I made to Germany on behalf of my study of Nazi doctors (late 1977). I was just getting into the study and it was a preliminary trip, but on that trip I managed to interview a few Nazi doctors as well as some survivors and immersed myself into a lot of things during a short trip of a few weeks. When I came back to New York after that trip, I had a strange reaction of my own. Of course, I talked to my wife about it a lot. But in terms of other relationships and social experiences it was very hard for me, because I couldn't talk to anybody about it. I felt nobody could grasp what I had been through and I couldn't not talk about it. Nothing else seemed important or immediate or worth saying to me. One way that I helped myself to make this transition was with my then editor and also friend. I sat down and had a drink with him and we had a long two-hour session, and I poured out to him, almost nonstop, what I had seen, what it meant to me, why it was so fascinating and evil and important, and some of what I had been through in learning about it and in immersing myself in the experience of what Nazi doctors did, and the experience of victims, and all of what I was beginning to study. That could be called something on the order of (mild or not so mild) posttraumatic experience which I had to come out of. But it also was, as a posttraumatic experience can be, the beginning of something to me very profound—some kind of knowledge that was conveyed to me with cost. We don't get away without cost from such an experience. Something was being conveyed to me by survivors that had elements of insight and some kind of wisdom that I was struggling to perceive through my work with Nazi doctors.

So getting back in a roundabout way to your question, the potential understanding or wisdom has to do with death and what people do under the threat of death; and what people do in connection with suffering and pain; and also evil, what people do in connection with evil, in perpetrating it and in being victimized by it. And, for the investigator of these issues, you can't learn anything or convey anything—you can't do anything right, valuable research or investigation—unless you open yourself to it and let that pain and suffering and evil enter into your own experience, into your own imagination.

GIAMO: In a similar way, when Jeff and I were down on the Bowery doing fieldwork in the late 1970s, about a year or so went by before we began to open ourselves up to a deeper encounter with the homeless men. And we began picking up on other images and themes which included this whole feeling of death, both the physical threat of death and kind of a lingering social death and a sense of disillusionment and despair—all amid the life that went on there. There was some very vibrant life that animated this setting, yet the deeper undercurrents were there. We evolved into this and it was a very profound experience for both of us. We could not remain the same afterward.

LIFTON: Yes, exactly; that's right, of course you couldn't.

GRUNBERG: By now I've come to know so many hundreds of homeless people and, as we talk about selective numbing, there are times I'll be sitting at home away from it all and there will be something on television that will display a composite of my feelings. In an instant I'll become very emotional. Then I have to change the channel, leave the room, not think about it.

LIFTON: We make a Faustian bargain, a devil's bargain. And I even try to convey this to my students who are involved in this kind of work. The Faustian bargain goes something like this: we allow ourselves, indeed know that we require a certain right to move in and out of the experience. That is, you two are with the homeless a certain amount of the time. You lived with them; the homeless are still in you. But you also allow yourselves the right to have some pleasures, some joy—wives, girlfriends, children, whatever. In fact, it's no surprise to learn psychologically that elements of love and even sensuality are more intensely required as a kind of counter to the death-dominated experience, whether it's with Hiroshima survivors or Nazi survivors or the homeless.

GRUNBERG: Our lucky wives.

L I F T O N: I once heard someone speak during my travels when I worked with Nazi doctors (we both were speaking at a conference at the time). And this person that spoke was both a rabbi and a Jungian analyst and he was himself a survivor of the Nazis. He had become a rabbi and a Jungian analyst working with survivors and, not only that, in his temple he had more or less sessions with survivors and he also volunteered to work in the Jewish community where he lived in a special way— volunteering to handle the dead. It's an ancient form of volunteering in Jewish communities, I'm told, which is a very special way of giving your-self to the community. And he gave his talk, which was quite interesting and mentioned all of these things. At the end of the talk I took him aside and said, "Your talk was very profound and very moving and I learned a lot from it and felt a great deal in listening to it. But I have to ask you how can you personally manage it. I've been studying Nazi doctors and trying to have a balance; it's not easy; it's been painful, but I just can't imagine what enables you to deal with it." And he looked at me and he said, in clearly articulated British South African tones, "I fuck a lot."

In further answer to your question about insight, it occurred to me just as we were talking here now that the homeless are like survivors who have what has been called "second victimization" or what Kai Erikson called in relationship to Buffalo Creek survivors the "second death." Take Hiroshima survivors. They may be a better comparative group. Hiro-shima survivors came to be viewed as victims because they experienced the bomb. The second victimization was their being made into outcasts, and that was very profound. I wrote about that and, in a way, it's any process of blaming the victim. But it's very important and it's important to hone in on it in a very detailed way. What it means psychologically is that you undergo the death immersion, let's call it, or the disaster that makes you a survivor in the first place. And that has a whole series of reverberations, almost all of them painful. And then society takes you and relegates you symbolically to the living dead in some way. So that's why I called my book *Death in Life*—the living dead in some symbolic sense. You are as if dead; you carry the death taint.

And it's part of my theory (to move from immediate group to theory) that victimization in general entails some kind of imposition of the death taint on the group that is victimized. They are one's designated victims. My theory is that many societies develop a designated victim, a group of people who serve them psychologically by becoming that and then the designated victim is as if dead. Therefore, when killed the designated victim can be killed readily since one is not killing a living human being. But that becomes very important because then with the second victimization some of the elements of the first victimization (their being immersed in death, their carrying death imagery within them) become connected with the process of the second victimization. It's easier to see them as death-tainted, as living dead or as nonliving dead, in some symbolic way because of what they've been through and, therefore, one can victimize them further, wash one's hands of them. In various ways, actual or symbolic or by neglect, one can really thrust upon them a very powerful second victimization, and I see the homeless as having that happen to them.

G I A M O: What I find remarkable in regard to survivors, and the homeless in particular, is that, despite what seems to be in many cases complete separation, stasis, and disintegration (to use your framework), there is this capacity to go on. There is a capacity to live, to create to some extent, to stay physically alive and, to a certain degree, socially and symbolically alive.

L I F T O N: Yes, that is interesting and important to say because they're living the life of survivors, and living it perpetually and, more or less, staying alive against the odds, you might say.

G I A M O: Does that speak for an almost innate human propensity for survival, for self-preservation?

L I F T O N: Certainly, in work I've done with victim-conscious survivors, one finds that tendency—the struggle to live and to find a way to mobilize their own death encounter in relation to their survival. Probably this could be said of the homeless in ways that you two could articulate better than I could.

G I A M O: If I may refer to our interview with Jerzy Kosinski, he would say that the homeless person must be a protagonist in his or her own dramatic predicament. In other words, one must use whatever condition one finds oneself in (of course, we're speaking here of the very bottom of the social system) and use it in some way to perpetuate one's life and to create, to some extent, to mobilize one's resources.

LIFTON: Yes, that's right, because becoming a protagonist means to be active, to take a stand, as opposed to a passive victim. But I think that the homeless may struggle with how much they can be a protagonist and how much they see themselves as stuck.

I wanted to say something more about this other issue of second victimization. It's easy for us, especially those of us with theories, to condemn the rest of society for its way of dealing with the homeless, and justly so, because they (the rest of society) deal badly with them. But again we have to start with ourselves. What are we doing? I'm sure that both of you, who have come closer to empathy for and, more than that, sympathy for the homeless (at least many of them), also often get angry at them. I know I get angry at them without knowing them at all and others simply get angry at them and condemn them. If I were to describe my own reaction, it alternates between the widely shared resentment of them and the kinds of thoughts I've been conveying to you about their victimization and empathy for them and sympathy for them and their plight. I react with resentment because they make me feel so uncomfortable by constantly confronting me with their pain, their victimization, in ways that make me feel guilty, and I don't have a ready solution to this. (So that's cause enough to make me resent them.) But the resentment felt by society is felt by all of us in some degree and one has to start with that realization. At the least, we share a double feeling, an ambivalence.

GRUNBERG: Could you define the concept of the protean style and do you see it as diametrically opposed to the homeless situation?

LIFTON: No, it mixes in with the homeless situation. By the protean style, or the protean self, I mean what I now take to be a *modus vivendi* for our times, the contemporary self (particularly but not exclusively the contemporary American self) characterized by fluidity and multiplicity— by changeability. And that can mean a sequence of immersion in a particular set of activities of a group of people or a particular set of beliefs and leaving one for another with relatively little psychological cost. Or that can also mean the simultaneously protean, simultaneously multiple images and tendencies that are often contradictory or antagonistic to each other. Or another sense of this is what I call the proteanism of everyday life, that is, the great social differences in the self-presentation people display in any particular institution or place or work place. All these are forms of proteanism.

I'm now immersed in this subject as my main research effort for the book that I'm working on now. I'm looking at actual people—the life studies of four groups that we are investigating at our center [Center on Violence and Human Survival at John Jay College and City University]. The four groups are fundamentalists, social activists, civic leaders, and what we originally called the black underclass (now we're calling that group underprivileged African Americans). We have a few homeless, incidentally, in that last group. Proteanism operates in all of these groups.

In the fundamentalists it's surprisingly present—surprising because I had always thought of fundamentalism as the antithesis of proteanism. In many ways it is; it's the desire to stand still or return to the past in various ways. But many fundamentalists are quite protean in spite of the doctrine they seek to focus themselves in or to embrace absolutely. And even in that they're a little bit protean because they can't quite believe in their own theology. For various reasons they have some doubts about the end-time version of their theology. Some fundamentalist preachers assert or imply that it's desirable to welcome nuclear holocaust because it would then be the realization of the biblical prophecy as writ in the Book of Revelation. In any case, some of the followers can't quite accept this theology and they hem and haw and modify it in a slightly protean way. In any case, the fundamentalists show proteanism.

The social activists are of course protean; we expected that. We know that in various ways, in their forms of activism, in their resistance to dogma, and in lots of other ways. That's no surprise. The civic leaders are quite protean. That was kind of a surprise. They believe in institutions and try to change them and they can be quite innovative and highly protean in different ways.

But when it came to the underclass, or severely disadvantaged, what's tragic and rather consistent is that the proteanism that at least has the possibility of serving other groups quite well (it has always had its pitfalls and potential dangers having to do with diffusion in some ways) tends to combine with an already existing fragmentation which is profound and, therefore, intensifies the fragmentation. In many cases that we see before us from these interviews, this leads to the most pained forms of dissociation and still deeper fragmentation.

For instance, some of the underprivileged African Americans that we interviewed in prison (on Rikers Island) frequently were people who went back and forth from being bright, very sensitive, rather articulate, and highly intelligent, with all kinds of interesting images about nuclear threat and end-time (which was part of the focus of the study), into being street toughs who had killed or had been violent or who had very direct unfeeling reactions to violence. And this switch happened right after the same person had talked with considerable feeling and sensibility and concern about other human beings and showed empathy, and so on. So the fragmentation and dissociation are deep. Of course, there are some among them who may extricate themselves from that group and we know of some of them who were headed for that and somehow extricated themselves from that fate and used the death immersion (which in one way or another, literally or figuratively, is just that when you're in the underclass, certainly in many of the black ghetto areas). They extricate themselves from that and go on to some form of realization, and again use their survival with some wisdom. But, more often than not, the fragmentation is deepened by the very proteanism.

The proteanism involves access to all kinds of imagery, including all the shallow imagery from society—the television and the consumer culture, and also some of the political images of liberalism or conservatism, the violent images of our society (many dimensions of which are put forward by television), some of the literary images, just about everything. Since proteanism is characterized by new combinations, it could help some people who have extricated themselves from homelessness because one of the cultural aspects of proteanism is that it can help you escape from and move out of dead ends, whether ideological dead ends or dead ends in one's mode of living, and toward alternative ideas and ways of living. The two of you have lived out certain degrees of proteanism, as have I, even in questioning your profession or combining professional knowledge with certain forms of social experience in becoming the kinds of people that you are, the kinds of scholars, activists, writers that you may be—all that. So proteanism can help people who have these threatening life exposures, but more often than that, in connection with many of the underclass, or underprivileged in this definition, it contributes to fragmentation.

GIAMO: In terms of protean culture, do you feel that many people are simply swamped by the intense fragmentation that we see? I know you have a phrase that was very vivid for me—the "flooding of imagery," which speaks to the effects of the mass media revolution.

LIFTON: It's an unavoidable part of the whole structure, part of the whole protean entity. Proteanism emerges from three major historical forces. First is what I call the breakdown of traditional symbol systems and the dislocation that results. The second is the mass media revolution, which is crucial to what we're talking about now. And the third is what I call the imagery of extinction or apocalyptic imagery—doing ourselves in as a species.

The dislocation, or the breakdown of traditional symbol systems, helps open up the self into receptivity to all kinds of images and the mass media make the images available. All of us feel inundated and a lot of the life we live, a lot of the psychic energy that we have, is expended trying to keep things out. Now, to some extent that's universal. Freud and others have written that the function of the human brain is just as much keeping things out as it is letting things in. It's always been that way, but with great intensification during the whole twentieth century and especially throughout the last half of it. So this sense of being flooded is part of the protean scene. And what I emphasize much more now in my recent work on proteanism is the need for structure and form, some balancing act between capacity for change and fluidity and form, or forms, and structure. The problem is that you can't just pick up on some old ideology or old institution or old custom. It doesn't usually work. We often find something beautiful in an old custom or old ideology and we'd like to have some of that quality, but it doesn't quite connect or feel genuine when it's transplanted fully into our contemporary systems. That's where one has to put together various elements or pieces, again new combinations. We're all doing that all the time.

GRUNBERG: And if a homeless person's starting point is fragmentation and disarray and social disconnectedness, he or she will be less likely to deal with this flooding in a way that is of benefit.

L I F T O N : That's right, because one needs some sources of strength to do that. I'm extraordinarily impressed by one man whom I interviewed among civic leaders. He's a very prominent person in the international human rights area. And just to make a long life story very brief, he told me a story of having been violently brutalized by his father when he was a young child, beaten and abused, and he went through all kinds of vicissitudes. And he was somehow able to transmute this victimization into a deep concern for all victims worldwide in his work on human rights. He did this through lots of elements that he doesn't fully understand by any means even now, and I certainly don't fully understand but learned a lot from talking with him. But he had to have certain sources of strength, some of them indirect, some of them hidden, some of them still unknown, for him to be able to do this—some sources of structure. And it had to do, in his case, with some nurturing he had somewhere from others besides his father, help from an extended family, which can be very important in such a case. The affirmation he received from certain teachers and an evolving capacity to create his own forms, his own self-process, enabled him to take advantage of those teachers and that help.

All of this came together in what could be called a protean transmutation or transformation of the most vicious form of trauma and betrayal as a child into a valuable quality and set of activities. And many of the homeless would be without that source of strength or structure or nurturing. But some will be able to call upon something. And, of course, a lot depends upon what we, you, the rest of us offer them.

G I A M O : In terms of self-process, what the homeless do have is their very homelessness, especially if this state of homelessness turns into a chronic condition. And it's very difficult to take that sense of identity away from a person without some repercussions. We have seen a certain arrogance in the presupposition that homeless people will want to, or be able to, give up their homelessness. In this sense, even after they become adequately sheltered, they may remain "homeless." An attachment to their suffering seems to have occurred. In your work, you have explored suffering as it affects identity and self-process. Could you discuss this—the relationship suffering people have with their own suffering?

LIFTON: Near the end of the Vietnam War (in 1975) there was the announcement that all Americans were leaving Vietnam. I'd pretty much stopped my work with Vietnam veterans by that time, but I was still in touch with some of the antiwar veterans. And one of the antiwar veterans I had been quite close to called me and said, "This announcement has really hit the guys very hard. They're really struggling with it now and a lot of them are really hurting about it. Would you like to talk with us?" I said, "Oh, yes, I would very much." We called together a group in my office (I was then at Yale) and we just chatted. We had another kind of rap group for a couple of hours, just a few of us, and we talked about their anger because what they suspected was all too true now—the whole thing had been useless, pointless. Everything they did meant nothing.

There are several things one can say about them that you can see right away have reverberations for the homeless. Survivors need as much as anything a meaning structure for their survival, for their death immersion, without which the rest of their lives can have little meaning. And with Vietnam veterans, if they became antiwar veterans, their main meaning structure from that painful death immersion had to be the very meaninglessness of their war which they could then declare to the whole American population as they tried to in becoming an activist group. And they did this brilliantly in a symbolic way with that marvelous and powerful and effective action of throwing their medals back in the face of those who had given them to these vets on the Capitol steps.

Well, I talked with them about all this and we discussed, as we had before in rap groups in earlier years, how long one goes on being an antiwar veteran or a Vietnam veteran in general. And they had heated discussions back and forth: "I'm tired of being defined as a Vietnam veteran. I'm a human being. I'm a student. I'm going to school. I'm a husband. I'm trying hard to be a good worker. I'm not just a Vietnam veteran." And another one said, when somebody asked, "How long are you going to be a Vietnam veteran?": "I guess I'm going to be a Vietnam veteran all my life." They were caught between these two poles.

I'm sure many of the homeless are similarly caught. I'm sure that many of them resent being simply a homeless person as a definition, as not quite a human being. On the other hand there's something in that kind of sense of self or identity, whether it's an antiwar veteran, a Hiroshima survivor, or a survivor of a Nazi death camp, that's very important. You've seen that many survivors of death camps keep their numbers tattooed on their arms. They can have it taken off. It wouldn't be that difficult. You can have a little surgical procedure and get rid of it. They keep it on there, and these other groups keep their identity of that kind of survivor.

I remember how stunned I was at some Auschwitz survivors. One of them—a Polish survivor—said to me, "You know, as horrible as it was I would not want to have missed it." I was unsettled by that comment, and I thought, she was Polish and not Jewish. Maybe since she wasn't Jewish she could have said that, because she also had a certain privileged position in the camp, relatively, although she suffered considerably, as did all Poles in camps. But then I heard a Jewish survivor say the same thing: "I wouldn't have missed it." And that unsettled me too. And not many said that. But others said, "Of course it was terrible, but it had a lot of value for me too." Many said that.

I'm getting at a certain mixture of pride, a sense of wisdom, a sense of having been through something and knowing something that others haven't been through and can't know, which I'm sure the homeless share. It has to be deeply ambivalent. And there's the very important and perhaps more obvious principle that in order to give up an identity one has to have another one in order to replace it. And that isn't so evident in many of these people.

Vietnam veterans would also talk about what they didn't like in Vietnam and then how they were struggling to become human again, as I said before. And they came to this recognition that on the one hand they'd like to renounce what they had been and done in Vietnam because they were almost a different person now and struggling to become a different person. On the other hand, as they tried to be honest with themselves, they realized and pointed out very strongly to one another: "That was me in Vietnam—I can't sever that dimension of myself from myself; I was that person." One of them showed very powerful slides which he developed as a slide sequence for various veterans' groups and others in the country. But in some ways one of the most powerful slides was a picture of himself as a marine with his chest out and looking very macho with his weapons, with a big gun right there. He was showing us the person he had been but no longer was. It's the doubling I speak of in my work which anybody goes through in basic training. Anybody comes out of basic training with some amount because basic training is a means of creating a pattern of doubling and converting the ordinary civilian person into the killer—one reason why it's so difficult to make the transition at all. But any case, that was one's self, that was part of one's self and you cannot give it up that easily. The healthy pattern is to reintegrate it into a more inclusive sense of self that still has a place for it. Otherwise one is in a different form of dissociation, so to speak.

In the case of the homeless, which I don't know first hand at all, I suspect that they're struggling to retain all of these elements, including the pride of the survivor, the inability to form an alternative identity (at least rather readily), and struggling with a way of integrating their sense of being homeless and maybe their critique of society in their own way—however articulate or inarticulate it may be. It's like saying, "I don't necessarily want to be just what you are. I may like a bed or a place to lie down, but that doesn't mean I want to become like you; and all you can offer me is the full package. I'm not sure I want the full package." Something like that.

GRUNBERG: In the Bowery they used to tell us that "you can't spell bum without 'u' in it."

GIAMO: Those skid row men expressed many social critiques and, whether rationally or irrationally stated, they were always compelling.

LIFTON: Yes, it's as if having in one sense opted out, or having been forced out, they construct a shared sense of self that separates them from the rest of us.

GIAMO: Perhaps it's analogous to what you call the "retirement phase." Whether they were forced out, or however they got there, they have retired from mainstream social life and can reflect on it.

LIFTON: Yes, they might even reflect on mistakes they've made before they became homeless. And after they reflect they may change their perspectives about themselves and society.

GRUNBERG: And many of them were almost immobilized by what they said would happen one day. One day I'll get back, one day I'll change. They were almost being comforted by the fact that they knew one day it would all change again, although they often did nothing about making that day happen. It's enough to know that one day it will happen.

LIFTON: When you said that I had a strange (or not so strange) association. You know, Judaism is famous for waiting for the Messiah. But I (and I'm not alone among Jews) have the theory that deep down the Jews don't want the Messiah to come because if the Messiah ever came what would we have to hope for? Yet we do need that image as a source of hope. But do we really want it to happen? There's some evidence one could say that we don't. At least we don't trust those who may complain. But it could be that the homeless who say they need the hope and yet really have some of the traits we've just been talking about are resistive to help because they can't find a way of integrating help into an evolving sense of self that they can themselves accept or respect.

GRUNBERG: In an earlier interview, Jerzy Kosinski said that, rather than blame society, he prefers to think of society as not being smart enough to solve the homeless problem. Similarly, he said that we can't blame the homeless individual, for if society isn't smart enough to resolve the problem of homelessness, why should we expect the homeless individual to be able to do so? What do you think of the process of assigning blame and its relationship to responsibility? Please consider the following: the blame put on psychiatry for the plight of the mentally ill homeless; greedy landlords and gentrification; and the government and adverse public policy decisions.

LIFTON: I guess the way I look at it is that maybe one should put aside the word "blame" and think about "responsibility." That is, I don't think we should simply let psychiatry or the city government or the federal government or the state government off the hook at all—or the greedy landlords. All these people should take some responsibility. Of course, I'm speaking, in part, of my own profession, although I'm an oddball psychiatrist no doubt. Responsibility for and to the homeless in some degree is important to consider. I, as a psychiatrist, didn't "create" homelessness. But insofar as I might have acquiesced in the delusion of solving the problem of mental illness by letting all the people with mental illness out of hospital care under the guise of progressive new ideas in psychiatry, then I share in that responsibility. More important than who is originally responsible is the responsibility right now. I think psychiatry as a profession could be saying something about the homeless and of course some people are. Some are saying some dubious things and a few may be saying some valuable things. And you can make a parallel kind of model for greedy landlords and all the administrations and perhaps especially the city. Certainly we do need federal programs about jobs and education and about various services which now are woefully insufficient (you people know that much better than I). You need to listen to the homeless themselves, for instance. There ought to be large forums with all these groups—with psychiatrists, with landlords (greedy or otherwise), leaders of the city, state, and national governments—about what's wrong and how to fix it, or at least how to improve the situation.

I wouldn't want to simply say that we're not smart enough to do it. We haven't been smart enough to do it yet. But being smart involves emotions, political positions, ethical commitments. So it involves a moral dimension, a professional dimension, and a political dimension, all of which have to be called forth. Some people know enough now to do valuable things and lots of others could soon learn enough to do or support very valuable programs. If a process were started or were expanded in which the homeless and those who worked closest with them could be allowed to convey to lots of others, including the groups I mentioned, more about the homeless state and directions of resolution or improvement of society, this could bring about a real change for the better.

G I A M O : In defining humankind as the "symbol-using, symbol-misusing animal," Kenneth Burke reminds us that humanity has the capacity for both conceptual regeneration and degeneration—the propensity to obscure as well as to illuminate. We have proposed that, in part, mystification (or the tendency to obscure) has gained the upper hand in society's response to homelessness. For example, despite the visibility of homelessness, extensive media coverage, intensive advocacy efforts, widespread volunteerism, government programs, and our familiarity as a people with this recurrent social problem, homelessness persists and an industry has grown up around it. How do you explain all this expenditure of energy with virtually no social transformation and none on the horizon?

LIFTON: Let me start with the first premise, which I agree with completely. Burke has always been a source of wisdom to me. Because we are the symbolizing animal we can symbolize or imagine virtually anything. What symbolization really means, in the sense that we're using it now, is recreating what we perceive and transforming that into virtually any kind of image or form. And these can be collective or individual or some combination thereof. Reasons for our destructive patterns of symbolizing homelessness are manifold. It isn't just that we mystify homelessness, which of course we do, but we mystify homelessness because of an already existing poverty of symbolization or already existing forms of mystification in our symbolization of political and social life—really everyday existence in our society. And to carry that idea further, we go through all sorts of maneuvers in order to try to be comfortable with our own sense of self, collectively and individually. So, in order to affirm our own virtue and our own achievements, we want to contrast it with the homeless. We want to see them as nonperformers. Above all, we want to put a wall between them and us.

Likewise, when I did my study of Nazi doctors some commentators were most angry at me for emphasizing how ordinary the Nazi doctors were rather than very special and innately evil, even though they did indeed become evil people. But in trying to build a wall between the homeless and ourselves that in turn limits the symbolization that we bring to homelessness. Other sources of limits involve the cruelty of certain innocent-sounding ideologies or ideological elements, such as the American ideology of free enterprise and the self-made man or woman—the Horatio Alger myth—readily transformed into let's say Republican politics: we don't "throw money" at problems. Therefore you would draw virtually all money from cities and from projects that involve job training, rebuilding of the ghettos, education, food for the poor, dimensions of help for enabling those who have been victimized to leave the designation of victim. The ideology sounds fine and self-justifying, but it's by one remove deeply cruel, even evil, given the level of need and the pain of victimization in our society. But that ideological baggage renders a lot of American symbolization of homelessness impoverished. So in that sense the mystification of symbolization of homelessness is directly parallel to the mystification of symbolization of nuclear weapons—of warmaking—and of the accompanying polarization of rich and poor in our society and the insensitivity to that polarization.

If you open up your symbolizing capacities, which is really opening up your imagination, then you can immediately see a kind of identification with the homeless in some degree, at least empathy for them. In a way, we all are a little bit, or not such a little bit, homeless. There is a kind of homelessness in the very proteanism I talk about or in our own confusions about ethical principles or about, really, grounding or roots—what we call roots. Which of us doesn't feel in some degree uprooted and uncertain about our grounding?

GIAMO: You have said that "the subjective experience of psychohistorical dislocation is precisely a sense of not having a place" [Lifton and Olson, *Living and Dying*]. Could you explain what you mean by psychohistorical dislocation and discuss its relevance to homelessness?

LIFTON: Really, psychohistorical dislocation is a form of spiritual homelessness. With that psychohistorical or more simply historical dislocation, each of us feels uncertain about the place formerly given people by the great symbols and institutions of existence—the symbols and institutions surrounding authority, religion, those of family, the life cycle, education. The structures and dogmas and symbols connected with all of these traditional forms are around but placed in considerable doubt, so we internalize them much more ambivalently if at all. In the face of that, we are uncertain about our place, our location, in connection with people, ethics, even geographically. Where should I live? Consider all the meanings of that question. You just have to stop and hear it and it means: where typically should my home be? Where should I exist? How should I exist? What should I believe? How should I bring up my children? Who should I help? To whom am I responsible? Who is responsible for me? Why should I live? All those questions seem to me pretty close to at least the experience of spiritual homelessness. I suppose we differ from the people on the streets in that we have an apartment or a house and a bed to come back to and we have made do in our own way with those questions rather imperfectly, but not much more than that.

GRUNBERG: Typically the black experience is very striking when we talk about dislocation. Slavery, of course, is certainly an example of this. Michael Harrington wrote of blacks as being America's "internal aliens" [*The Other America* (1962)] and James Baldwin wrote of himself as "a kind of bastard of the West" ["Autobiographical Notes" (1955)].

LIFTON: Yes, because the blacks in this country are what I would call the designated victims. In many parts of Europe the designated victims are the Jews. In this country it's been the blacks, and by that term (designated victim) I mean those upon whom a society or a majority of a society psychologically feeds. In that sense we have fed on the blacks not just economically—exploited them in that sense—but psychologically in that they've served certain psychological needs as a victimizing group. As I see it, to have the blacks as victims in a victimizing process is done by designating a victim as death-tainted. One can in that way reassert the life power of one's own group and the immortality—survivor immortality—of that group and feel more alive and more powerful. So for those reasons I think that blacks have indeed been "aliens" and, in Baldwin's terms, the "bastard[s] of the West" or of this country. And they've struggled painfully with relocating themselves psychologically and spiritually. It's not by coincidence that the book *Roots* (and the widely viewed television programs) came out of the black experience and the whole focus on blackness and negritude in other parts of the world as an aspect of that struggle.

GIAMO: In the introduction to one of your essays you refer to the Baldwin quote about being "caught in the teeth of history."

LIFTON: That's right, and what he meant by it and what I meant in quoting him is that we're all caught (some more than others) in the forces of history. Some are more "in" the bite than others, and that's certainly true of blacks in this country. In a way one could say that the homeless are in the teeth of history now. That really means that certain historical and then social forces come together for certain groups to lock them into being bitten or nearly eaten by destructive instruments.

GRUNBERG: In New York City, 70 to 80 percent of the homeless population is black.

LIFTON: Well, that's a staggering figure in itself. One is both staggered and unsurprised I would say. That's my reaction. It's a very telling figure and by no means a surprise. One would say similar statistics about prison I guess, and for similar reasons.

GIAMO: About 46 percent of all federal prisoners around the country are black.

LIFTON: So it's not as extreme but a similar principle is at work.

GRUNBERG: Do you think an argument can be made that perhaps America owes restitution of some sort, designated restitution to blacks? Is restitution possible?

LIFTON: Restitution on the part of the American people and American government is both impossible and necessary. What I said is self-evident: it's impossible in the sense that you can't undo slavery or its effects and the victimization following slavery of the blacks. But necessary in that there is a responsibility toward blacks. That's why we should not abandon all the attempts at programs that try to favor blacks or speak to the black condition. And that, of course, is a matter of the responsibility I spoke of. You can't renounce responsibility toward any group in this country that is radically disadvantaged, and that's a very mild word for what people go through. And that's true of no larger group than the blacks.

GRUNBERG: For you personally, what has been so compelling about being near to people who have suffered and survived? How has your work affected your life?

LIFTON: There are deep satisfactions in working with survivors and with people who have been through death immersion, pain, suffering. The satisfaction has to do with a kind of knowledge and insight, a kind of wisdom, that one derives. It has to do with a sense that one has done something or is doing something that's profoundly difficult and has opened up an aspect of oneself, at least opened it up partially, that had been closed—that part of oneself having to do with openness to death and suffering. One has more respect for oneself in doing this.

And then there's a kind of self-interested aspect here, which I say in a nonderogatory way. That is, once one develops as investigator and activist, a sense of oneself as a person who can do this work and who knows something about this kind of work for whom it is right to do this work emerges. And then one goes on doing it. So that people would say to me, "How could you possibly take on a subject like the Nazi doctors? You must have been very brave. It must have taken a lot of courage." And I knew that I felt no sense of bravery or courage and that wasn't it at all. It was rather a sense that at a certain moment in my life it was right for me. That comes from a combination of previous experience and a sense of what one is able to do, a sense of what one believes one is able to do. And we struggle very hard all of our lives to understand what's right for us. In a simple way, in academic life, or in any form of work, one of the hardest questions to answer is what one wants to do. I've had various young people come and talk to me and ask me how to get a grant or something like that. And I ask them: what do you really want to do? It's a very hard question to answer. When you come to some sense of what you want to do, what speaks to your own condition as a human being—and that constellation has to do with suffering and death—then one follows that path. And one realizes along the way one can give form to some of that suffering and death immersion—that's crucial. If you can't give form to it you'll just feel its pain and you probably won't stay with it. But it's the capacity to give some form to it and I mean, of course, form that has political and intellectual values.

Again, one has to speak personally. When I did my work investigating Nazi doctors there was great satisfaction and nurturing in working with survivors. Working with non-Jewish Germans who were anti-Nazis and very committed to my work meant a lot to me. That was a bond. I also felt a bond with fellow students of the Holocaust, many of whom had similar commitments and helped me a lot. But I was also helped by the recognition from the very beginning that I would write a book about this. In this case it was a form of revenge—an intellectual's revenge to write the book, to have one's say. But it was also a sense of giving form to something that had not been given form to in the same way, or to give a new form that had value in speaking out against a certain kind of cruelty.

And the image of writing a book helped me get through a lot of pain. Just as I suspect the image of either writing about or contributing to certain programs that will help the homeless now helps both of you to get through what you're experiencing.

GRUNBERG: It helps to draw birds.

LIFTON: Yes. That's the gallows humor. Gallows humor—I'm sure you find it among the homeless—is a very strong dimension of all this. It's part of the protean process, the protean style, but it's also a desperate need of anyone involved in this kind of work.

ROBERT W. RIEBER

Homelessness and
Social Distress

JEFFREY GRUNBERG: Do you know what you have on your block? You have a homeless soup kitchen one block down in the Park Avenue Church. We walked past it and the homeless were waiting outdoors to go in.

ROBERT RIEBER: Well, one of my favorite quotes about all this is Gandhi's statement to a news reporter when he was being interviewed. This news reporter asked him why he lived in such poverty. (Gandhi was weaving his own clothing and living like a real peasant.) And Gandhi chuckled and said, "My 'friends' tell me that it costs them a lot of money to keep me in poverty." And I think it's going to cost the government a lot of money to keep the homeless in homelessness. Until they get them out. Just like it cost the government a lot of money to bail out the homeless, it's the same with the savings and loans that are homeless. The banks are homeless because of mismanagement. And it costs us all a lot of money because of that. And the homeless are going to cost us a lot of money before it's all over. And the social stress from all this is going to aggravate a lot of people.

GRUNBERG: Are you saying that the goal is to spend money or that such expenditures create an industry?

RIEBER: Well, I stressed money only because I sensed that the debt of our times centers around the political economy of the world. And all you hear when you read the news or hear the news on the media is the way the debt is escalating and the way the problems of money are affecting everybody's lives. Whether it's jobs, or being able to pay the bills, or being able to do the everyday routine things of life. Money has become internationalized, especially with the event of the so-called victory over communism by capitalism. The Soviets now want to learn how to be capitalists, so we send them our experts and lend them our money.

BENEDICT GIAMO: To teach them about free enterprise, privatization, and management development?

RIEBER: Yes. But they don't understand money—in the market sense of the word "money."

GRUNBERG: So as long as money is being spent, society is moving on?

RIEBER: It's going to cost both public and private institutions a hell of a lot of money to keep these people in homelessness until you get them out. And how are you going to get them out? Nobody quite knows what they want.

GIAMO: Does the way in necessarily lead to a way out?

RIEBER: Well, there's always a way out. The question is whether or not one's wise enough to find it.

GIAMO: I was thinking about the shelter systems in major cities. Take New York City for instance. Twelve years ago (in 1979), in the landmark case of *Callahan* v. *Carrey*, shelter was determined to be a right and the city, based on a consent decree, stepped up its efforts in providing shelters for the homeless. On the one hand, the extensive shelter system has provided eleventh-hour emergency relief for the homeless; yet, on the other hand, by institutionalizing disenfranchisement, the system has aggravated the social problem. In short, the massive, depersonalized shelter systems have perpetuated the very thing they were designed to alleviate. And it becomes increasingly difficult to see a way out of the current labyrinth of public shelters.

RIEBER: Well, I don't know what it means to see a way out. Naturally when you're looking to get out—when you're lost—you don't know how to find your way out. When you're lost you don't see your way out, but in the process of searching for a way out you eventually find it if you put your mind to it, or you're up a creek. I'm assuming there is a way out.

GIAMO: Why haven't we found it so far? Is it strictly money? Or does it have something to do with social attitudes and perceptions?

RIEBER: Well, it took a long while to get into this problem and I don't think it's solvable instantaneously.

GRUNBERG: But isn't that really the meaning of the Gandhi quote?

RIEBER: I don't think the problem is fully acknowledged at this point, and that's why we're in a big hole. I think that denial is the massive problem which we're inflicted with today. I don't even think we've made the first step in accepting the problem as it really is. So in that sense some people don't even think that we're in trouble enough to acknowledge that they are lost. Consequently, they don't look for a way out. If that's what you're talking about, the answer is yes.

GRUNBERG: And many homeless people are not looking for a way out of homelessness. It is often accepted by many as their natural course.

RIEBER: Well, I think homelessness was their way out at a certain point. The homeless found their way out by developing the condition of homelessness. Their way out of the social infrastructure, out of the establishment, that was the homeless' way out. So if their way back in is to go back into the social infrastructure that they wanted to get out of, naturally, they don't want any part of it.

GIAMO: But what is the degree of intentionality? From the way you're talking it sounds as if the homeless have maximum choice to move in and out of society at will.

RIEBER: I'm not suggesting a plot that the homeless got together in back of 79th Street and the cavern underneath the marina and planned it. They are on the fringe end of society. They've broken off from a subculture, from lots of different subcultures. No longer do they belong to the main culture or any of the subcultures, and they are in the process of forming their own subculture. So what we see here is a new subculture emerging from society. That means that they want out of whatever they were in. And to the extent that they have gotten out they probably feel satisfied that they're out; they may not be satisfied with the condition that they're in, but it's the lesser of two evils. "I'd rather be out of the establishment and down-and-out homeless than be back in the establishment."

GRUNBERG: So we're not talking so much about people who for the first time ever, due to some crisis, descend into homelessness. This incidence of homelessness might only last several months' time spent in a Red Cross shelter until the victims' homes are rebuilt. What we're really talking about are people whose lives unravel over and over again, despite seeming opportunities, and they spend most of their time living in homelessness, year after year after year.

RIEBER: Well, I imagine that if you stated my case you would get a different story from each person. But there must be a common thread to these people to the point where if you got John Jones here and said, "OK, now why are you a homeless person? Don't you want to stop being homeless?" And then you give him the way out, which is going right back into the condition that he was in before. "You want me to get a job in that cockamamie place and go through all that shit again? That's what I just went through and you want me to go back in there again and go through the same thing all over again?"

GRUNBERG: Well, you have to be less transient—you have to do this and you have to do that. And you're saying they may not accept all that goes along with this and they may go through the motions halfheartedly.

RIEBER: They seem to be willing to accept the condition that they're in now, whatever that might be. They're happy if you accept them in that condition and if you give them the necessary means of existence to survive in that situation. Because they perceive it to be dangerous if they make a move either forward or backward. They certainly know that they don't want to go back where they came from. You can't go home again.

GIAMO: But, socially, where did they come from?

RIEBER: Well, I really don't know where they came from.

GIAMO: I mean in terms of our class system?

RIEBER: I really don't know. I think that they must share some common denominator, having come from somewhere within the social infrastructure where it was so bad they couldn't make it. And that's what they share. I mean the down-and-out people who never had much of a home to begin with and could not find their way out of it. They may have been drug addicts. They may have had some contact with mental illness or a combination of both. At least that's what we seem to see in the population here in New York City. And that is certainly something that they share in common.

GRUNBERG: So what does that say for those who clamor about cause? That a lack of housing causes modern homelessness, or economic forces cause homelessness, or deinstitutionalization causes homelessness.

RIEBER: This word "cause" is the biggest weasel word around. I don't know what they mean by cause. If I had a strep throat and you took a culture from my throat and found a specific type of bacteria—and you knew that certain antibiotics would kill certain types of bacteria—and you gave me antibiotics and you killed this thing that caused the bacteria, and then you said, "I found the cause and I gave you the cure," well, then, all right. But I don't think you have that kind of operation working here. You're not going to find a single factor which has the power to produce the social disease of homelessness that we're talking about in that way. So you're talking about something different from that, which is probably more realistic, something like a whole interacting system of events which trigger off other events and then trigger off other events and keep interacting in ways that come together and build up. That's probably what happened over a long period of time. And to point to one single factor as the cause of the event is simplistic and deceiving.

GIAMO: So do you think that the problem of homelessness has been misstated?

RIEBER: Well, if one states it in such simplistic terms—x is the cause of y, get rid of x to get rid of y—then the answer is yes.

GRUNBERG: I guess "cause" takes on a political action meaning. If you scream that housing causes homelessness, then what might come of this is more housing. If you say a whole interaction system, it might freeze people in their place.

RIEBER: There is no question about the fact that the degree to which the housing problem was engineered in this city has exacerbated the quality and the quantity of the conditions of those people we call homeless. There's no doubt about that. If you didn't have such a housing crisis, you would still have homelessness, but it wouldn't be so exacerbated or so extreme in both quantity and quality of lifestyle.

GRUNBERG: You might even have homeless people living in apartments. Sometimes you can't take homelessness away from a homeless person; it's all that they have left. Though they might be living somewhere for a while, they might still be living like a person who is fundamentally homeless in the world. In a way, it relates to your play on words—the man who mistook his door for a home—which you derived from Oliver Sacks' book, *The Man Who Mistook His Wife for a Hat.*

RIEBER: Reminds me of that old limerick: I wish my room (or home in this case) had a floor. I don't care too much for a door. This walking around without touching the ground is beginning to be quite a bore.

GIAMO: Since we are talking about cause, in a recent piece one of the coalition advocates, Kim Hopper, stated that "homelessness is not a trait or a property or an affliction of persons; it is a circumstance that presents a distinctive problem, where to spend the night" [in Carol L. M. Caton (ed.), *Homeless in America* (1989)]. What's your understanding of this particular attribution of cause?

RIEBER: Well, I don't know that where to spend the night is the best way to put it. A lot of people that I know who have that problem of where to spend the night are not homeless. But I think I know what he means—that the homeless just don't have any place to go, no one to depend upon, least of all themselves. Probably in the final analysis what the homeless (in their own unique way) share with the rest of the world is a problem. It's the problem of individual responsibility to yourself. And, certainly, the homeless are unique in that respect because they have the problem of not being responsible for themselves enough to be able to maintain a home for themselves. The rest of the population of the world have various degrees of irresponsibility about themselves on other levels.

But that's at a rock bottom, grass-roots level of life, not to be able to make it. With your own home or by your own home I mean anyplace that you can go back to at night; it doesn't have to be the place where you live.

GIAMO: Are you saying that this is a failure on the part of homeless people—to be in the condition they're in today?

RIEBER: Well, I'm not trying to blame somebody. That doesn't do much good because blaming the poor for being poor or blaming the sick for being sick is simplistic and leads nowhere. It doesn't help anyone. That was not my intention. My intention was to zero into the human condition that recognizes the importance of an interaction process that has reciprocal responsibility at all levels within the system. A deficit, a condition lacking in the human being that if a person had it he or she might have a greater chance of getting out of this dilemma.

GIAMO: To what extent do social forces help determine or predetermine these types of problems and conditions?

RIEBER: Well, obviously, we live in the context of a social environment where there are multidimensional forces acting on us all the time. But I sense we're getting into that trap again as to who's to blame. It reminds me of that movie with Marlon Brando, *The Formula*, where one of his stooges comes up to him (Brando's playing this industrial head of a big oil company). He says to Brando, "The lines are so long out there to wait for gas; they're miles long; it's getting bad. Maybe we ought to lower the prices or make it more available because the blame is going to come to us. On the other hand, maybe we can blame it on the Arabs." And Brando looks at him, smiles, and says, "You don't understand, we are the Arabs." In a sense I might say, "What's the matter with you? We are the social forces." We are a part of those social forces as individuals as much as the social forces are alien to us as individuals. Without us they wouldn't be here.

GIAMO: Without us the homeless wouldn't be here.

RIEBER: Yes, without us the homeless wouldn't be here.

GRUNBERG: You recently wrote a book entitled *The Psychopathy of Everyday Life and the Institutionalization of Stress* [published by Basic Books] which deals with the problems of social distress. Could you discuss your notion of social distress and how it occurs to you that it might relate to homelessness?

RIEBER: Well, earlier I gave you an example of a piece of social distress: in effect, the way the members of Congress, although they were not the perpetrators as it were, created the means to produce the problem of this tremendous amount of money that the American public is going to have to pay off. And they did it in a way that I think outrages most people. They are saying that we have to pay a bunch of hoodlums who went into the saving and loan business knowing full well that there was no risk because they were setting it up to get bailed out by the government. They walked out the back door with the money, and now we're going to have to give the people back the money who were insured by the government. That's institutionalizing distress financially, socially, and politically, and to the point of absurdity and to the point where it could break the backs of the social structures and the people who hold them up. That's the meaning of social distress.

For other examples, take the health care system and the criminal justice system. If you were hit by hospitalization and litigation simultaneously, you'd have to be a Hercules to hold up under the amount of stress that those two institutions produce on the individuals that come into contact with them. Yet they were not set up to produce stress; they were set up to alleviate stress. The educational system creates people who go into the system, fail any number of times, and are pushed into high school, and then are pushed into college, and then fail out of that. And keep in mind that the mission of education was to give them the knowledge so that they could do the job that they were hoping to be able to do when they came out. There's two strikes against them. Instead of two assets, they have two strikes against them. One more and they're out. That's what's happening with education. These are major and fundamentally important institutions within the culture. And if they don't function properly, the culture's going to go down the drain.

GRUNBERG: What makes for these kinds of social distress?

RIEBER: Irresponsibility, ignorance, lack of planning, and lack of care and concern. Those are the problems that give birth to the kinds of situations I've just mentioned. Greed and irresponsibility are at the bottom of it all.

GIAMO: Has it always been rampant? You can look back down through the 1980s and even back to a historical America and you would see signs of social distress, especially if you're looking at it in terms of irresponsibility, ignorance, and corruption.

RIEBER: I think you're right. There has been a good deal of social distress within the heritage of the United States of America and, to a certain extent, our national character has been built upon it. For example, two related phrases come to mind: "A sucker is born every minute" and "Never give a sucker an even break." That's the dark side. We have a brighter side too which doesn't seem to be coming forth at the moment to meet the demands of the situation. We're still hoping that Superman is going to fly in at any minute and just wipe the whole problem out. This exemplifies too much dependency and irresponsibility.

GIAMO: In his book *People of Plenty*, David Potter wrote extensively about the national character. His own particular analysis looked at the integral roles of technological innovations and economic development as setting the pace for more affluent standards of living. Do you see this as somehow being part of the context in which social distress then develops?

RIEBER: I think that's part of the picture. I'm not against technology. I'm concerned, deeply concerned, about the extent to which technology, artificial intelligence, and the computerization of humankind can lead to the shirking of responsibility that's necessary for human beings to decide upon their own destiny. I'm not sure whether we know who will survive. Human beings as we know them, or artificial intelligence which can produce machinelike human beings, pose real threats to the life of the mind. And I have no doubt that the extent to which artificial intelligence can grow might shock us all in the future. That's what worries me, because I don't think that scientific and technological advancement is bad. But, to the extent that we shirk responsibility by giving to technology that power to do the work for us, we may find ourselves in a position where we no longer have trained young people to take on the tasks that are necessary to get them through. Then we run the risks of becoming the victims of a Frankenstein monster that we have created unwittingly.

GIAMO: Kenneth Burke is fond of saying that "mankind is rotten with perfection." Referring to just what you're describing—the quest for the new, for the improved, for progress, the addition to scientific knowledge, which on the backside causes such a rupture in our ability to keep up and to use that newness in productive ways to advance human values.

RIEBER: I'm sure that someday somebody is going to tell us that artificial intelligence is what's needed to solve homelessness, if it is still around ten years from now to the extent that it is now.

GIAMO: Homelessness has been around this country in large-scale urban environments ever since the 1870s. In one way, it's been constant for over 100 years and, in other ways, of course, the forms of homelessness have changed. What do you say about a social problem that has been so persistent over the years?

RIEBER: I'm sure that everything you say is correct. My reaction, however, is that there is something fundamentally and extraordinarily different today about the problem of homelessness than I can ever remember in my lifetime. Admittedly, I'm better off now than I was ten years ago and ten years ago I was better off than I was ten years before that. And I'm not a youngster anymore. I've been in this field for the past thirty years or so. I can remember when I went to Europe and I saw the first person that I had ever seen in rags. He was in Ireland, and I said, "Ahhh, now I know where Dickens got this idea of people in rags." I'd never seen anybody in rags. Now, that may have been the surprise response of someone from a privileged situation, but I wasn't all that privileged. I lived in pretty ordinary conditions in Philadelphia. And I wasn't brought up with a silver spoon in my mouth. I never saw anybody in rags. Nowadays it's the other way around. Europe's never seen anybody in rags. But when

Europeans come here they see them all over the place, not only people in rags but people who are worse off both mentally and physically. So there's something about today that is different in comparison to right after World War II. And now it's produced a situation which strikes one so strongly that it sticks out like a sore thumb, and you can't help but recognize and be appalled by it—especially when you figure into the equation the extraordinary progress that has been made that should come back to the people in benefits. So, yes, it's been around but it disappears and comes back in another form, so it looks like it's new.

GRUNBERG: Considering your notion of institutions not being as supportive as they ought to be, maybe it is a concept of three strikes you're out. And maybe the homeless have struck out three times: in the first few years of life, a breakdown of the family, then schools that aren't working, and then perhaps drugs or violence entering the scene, and involvement with the criminal justice system. By the time they are of an early age they've struck out a few times and now they're out.

RIEBER: They're not even on the team anymore. They're not receiving any pay and they don't have a home to live in. And they don't want to come near all the pain and the structure that came into power. They don't want to be part of that league any more. They want to start their own new league and to hell with that league where the pain was felt. Now they have no hope, only fear and despair.

GRUNBERG: Well, they get booed. They just come up to plate and they get booed. So why not form another team? I want to show you this cartoon. It nicely describes some aspects of social distress that you've been talking about. [The *New Yorker* cartoon, from July 16, 1990, shows a corporate board room with eight lifeguards seated around a square conference table. All of them are wearing tank top shirts; the director has a whistle strung around his neck. One of the lifeguards is standing and reading from a memo. The caption reads: "Under new business: Peterson, at Hammond Point Beach, reports that a person in the water is flailing about and calling for help. Peterson wants to know what action, if any, he should take."]

RIEBER: That's very good, and I can make up the next caption. After ten minutes of deliberation, they decide that this committee isn't large enough to make the decision and it will have to be passed on to a larger committee. The lack of personal responsibility is inherent in that whole operation.

GRUNBERG: In other words, once the problem is recognized, perhaps there's some responsibility we have in intelligently attending to the problem.

RIEBER: Yes, I think people are genuinely afraid of taking responsibility for their actions. They have been taught by policy, and by the actions of that policy, that it's dangerous to do so. Some even feel that it's dangerous to think about these things, especially if you do something good that interferes with somebody else's plans to make it bad. And they get heck for it several times and they say, "What the hell, I'm not going to do this again; I'm not going to stick my neck out. I saved that guy and now they're going to put me in jail for drowning him." Something like that. Why do you think mental doctors don't treat inactive people on the street these days?

GIAMO: Insurance?

RIEBER: Exactly. They'd be sued.

GRUNBERG: And they would be.

RIEBER: Yes. You're cutting your nose off your face when you create conditions like this—whereby people are not only afraid to help, but rationally they know why they shouldn't move in the direction of care and treatment. Because then you have no right to ask the question "Why are we destroying ourselves?" In effect, you have made the very conditions and policies that are right for self-destruction.

GRUNBERG: In discussing the problems the mentally ill face, you used a phrase that ironically summarized the history of the mental health system in the United States over the past century.

RIEBER: That's right. The mental health system started out as the nut-house, and then it progressed to the halfway house, and now it's turned into the outhouse. So we've gone from the nuthouse to the halfway house to the outhouse. And very few people seem to care enough to do very much about it.

GRUNBERG: How does the penthouse fit into your scheme? The old notion of poverty in the face of affluence.

RIEBER: You know the penthouse was a creation of the 1920s and 1930s, wasn't it? I don't know; I never thought about the meaning of penthouse. Of course, it's a status symbol of affluence and the very an-tithesis of the outhouse.

GRUNBERG: And those who live in them [penthouses] are the ones who have all that money to keep the outhouses built. I've enjoyed listen-ing to you talk about the relevance of the movie *The King of Hearts*. This might be a good time to bring it up.

RIEBER: Yes, it was a very popular movie in Cambridge. I think it had the longest run of any movie that ever played in Cambridge, Massachusetts.

GRUNBERG: The essence of the movie was that there were mentally ill people living as outcasts inside an asylum. It was set during World War I when the Germans were going to move into the city from one side and the British were going to move in from the other side . . .

RIEBER: And somehow there was a bomb one of them planted in the middle of the city and it was going to blow up the whole place. So all the people evacuated except for the mentally ill who were in the asylum. Then the British sent in a scout who was supposed to find and disconnect the bomb and let them know when the Germans were going to leave so that they could capture the city. And when he got into the city he saw nobody there. But then he stumbled upon the mental hospital. He walked in and appeared in front of the mentally ill, and they introduced them-selves as Napoleon, Churchill, and suchlike. Then they said, "Who are you?" And so, feeling like a nobody, he said, "I am the king of hearts."

And the mentally ill all bowed down and said, "We've been waiting for you for ages, sire; thank God that you've come to save us." And he was accepted by them and then they all made their grand exit out of the hospital and back into the city where they had come from before entering the hospital. The barber went back to the barbershop and the prostitute went back to prostitution. Now, since all the rest of the city was vacant, they were having themselves quite a ball. Well, the scout forgot about sending all those messages and the British army started coming in from one side and the German army from the other side. Both armies walked into the city and found all these mentally ill having a ball in the middle of the street. And then the armies started shooting at one another. Of course, the mentally ill went back into their hospital, and the British soldiers started chasing the Germans out of the city. Then the Brits beckoned to the scout that he should hop onto the truck. They threw him a helmet and a gun and you saw him running to catch the truck around the corner with his helmet and his uniform on. But then, after the truck turned, you saw that he didn't jump on after all. He threw away his helmet, stripped down naked, and banged on the door of the mental institution until they let him in.

GRUNBERG: I like listening to that story because there's a part of me that likes to romanticize homelessness as a social condition comprised of many people who have both intelligence and stamina and who, for their own best interests, decide to vacate the mainstream.

RIEBER: I don't really know whether they formally *decided* upon it as such. I really don't know. It's very hard to know what that process is all about. Maybe some have—with forethought and consideration—vacated the mainstream. But in a way I think that this would be completely alien to the ways in which we decide. It's more like the only decision they could make. It's not as if they had about four options: one to live in the penthouse, one to be homeless, and so on.

GIAMO: Yes, I agree. And that reminds me, perhaps Jean-Paul Sartre's point has been overstated: there does seem to be a way out—it's called *exit only*. The only catch is that its path happens to be one-way and down.

GRUNBERG: But isn't there a certain freedom to that exit? In *Down and Out in Paris and London*, George Orwell wrote that when you only have to worry about where your next meal is coming from, there's a certain sense of release in that bargain.

RIEBER: Yes, when you *only* have to worry about that prospect. Then all those other bothers that you had are gone.

GIAMO: You exchange a free-floating anxiety for a preoccupation with necessity and survival. Orwell's statement speaks for the difference between an existential or metaphysical homelessness and the social condition of homelessness we are bearing witness to today. I think back on that phrase—the man who mistook his door for a home—which, existentially, is tantamount to saying, "Where can I find *home* in the world?" The door appears as just another threshold and passageway to yet another construction of identity in our modern or "postmodern" consciousness. So that, as members of a very mobile American society, we're on the move, we're transient, and we'll always be hanging new doors to frame new formulations of ourselves as a people. So that makes us very unstable, very uprooted. And then you have the social and literal sense of homelessness, that is, the man who did *not* mistake his door for a home, but who is actually *using* his door as a home. Here you have the homeless with cardboard boxes, carrying their doors on their very backs, like a great social burden, drifting from city block to city block, moving through an environment that one observer has dubbed the "grate" society. And for these people the door is all there is; it's entirely detached from possibility.

RIEBER: The man who mistook his door for a home. I think that is a very accurate way of describing the norm of the modern or "postmodern" man.

GIAMO: I find it difficult reconciling the existential vision of homelessness with the literal and social phenomenon of people on the street, in transportation terminals, in abandoned buildings, shelters, and the like. It almost seems like a luxury to be speaking of metaphysical homelessness.

RIEBER: Yes, it's complicated. On the one hand, you have this guy who comes home and mistakes his door for his home because he doesn't see anything in his home that amounts to anything deeply spiritual or even worthwhile. It's only the bloody door that he's concerned with and he's got to make sure that it's locked every night so nobody else takes it. The other person might reach a point where she'll steal anything she can from anybody else's home or even just take something off the street if it's discarded and make her home out of that piece of junk.

GRUNBERG: And we do have transportation terminals filled with homeless people.

RIEBER: Yes, those grandiose stations which we discarded a long time ago have now become important symbols. That's very interesting because these great train stations and great post offices of the late nineteenth century often lie dormant. Some of them were actually destroyed and new structures built on the land where they once stood. But some of them managed to survive. And what has happened to them is quite interesting. In some cities, such as Union Station in Washington, D.C., they have been transformed into a combination of station and modern mall (with most of the old beauty preserved).

So these structures remain a living symbol of the past. Once the great trains and the transportation infrastructure supported the common people. Now they no longer exist because the train business is but a fraction of what it used to be, what it might be, and what it could become. By and large it was destroyed and then saved at the last minute, and now they're trying to build it up again. These are the urban spaces that we now use to put those people who don't have anyplace to go. And that's because there's nothing left in the architectural design of the modern city that's going to accommodate them. It's like throwing the homeless back into the past.

GIAMO: In light of this example, do you think that the problems of the homeless are integral to the problems of the broader American society?

RIEBER: In the final analysis one might say that homelessness today is one of the powerful symptoms of the moral decline of modern society.

GRUNBERG: The public's response to homelessness is now similar to what it was 100 years ago. We went to an exhibit—"On Being Homeless"—at the Museum of the City of New York that was on display a few years ago. And the presentation of paintings, lithographs, photography, and written documentation by social observers and the media made us think that American culture was reduplicating the symbolic landscape of homelessness in its current depiction of the social problem. For instance, the quotes from the work of Nels Anderson in the 1920s and 1930s made us feel as if he were talking about our present situation—the public response is minimal at best; there's not enough money to fund viable social and economic programs; agencies are lumping the mentally ill with the able-bodied homeless; the inability or unwillingness of teasing apart results from causes is leading to the mystification of the social problem. And so it goes, a perpetual state of social crisis. The Chinese have a saying that brings out the contradictory nature of crisis as both a danger and an opportunity. If you accept crisis as both a danger and an opportunity, then—within the American scene—what is the danger? And wherein lies the opportunity that our present crisis might be giving us?

RIEBER: Well, Dirty Dick Nixon wrote a book on that, didn't he? It was called *Six Crises*. In it he describes how he managed to profit by taking advantage of crisis situations that were dangerous. I'm not using Nixon as an example to us all. I deplore everything he stands for and especially the creation of his new presidential museum and the way the media covered it and made him look like a folk hero. It's ironic that a man who stood for all of the worst that we can imagine in leadership of a great nation like this can actually, in spite of himself, emerge in his latter years as a folk hero, even though that designation grossly misperceives the stature of the man and his public record. That's not to say that everything he did was wrong or bad, but when he did do right and good he usually did it for the wrong reasons, I'm sure.

But, certainly, within the notion of a crisis there is the element of danger in the sense that, if you don't handle it right, you can go down in the storm. And, if you do handle it right, you can collect the insurance for the damages, and then build up a new business. Crisis wakes up a lot of people who I think have become too secure and cocksure about what they have been doing. And in that sense it's both a danger and an opportunity, especially if you've fallen into the trap of complacency. Because then you can awaken to what you were doing in a way that you might not have awakened to before, thus renewing the process of correction and reform.

GIAMO: As a nation, do you think we are presently on the path toward an awakening and correction?

RIEBER: I think we're in the great sleep. Rather than the "Great Awakening," we're in the great sleep, the deep sleep. And we're dreaming all over the place. The media are giving us the social dreams—the symptoms of contemporary life—in order to alert us to the problems we have created that remain unresolved. But in a great sleep we don't recognize and properly interpret the messages we send to ourselves. There's no Great Awakening as Jonathan Edwards understood it.

GIAMO: Is part of the problem of the "great sleep" the fact that the social world today seems so fragmented, so complex, so pervasively opaque that it seems incomprehensible to the man or woman on the street, let alone to our political leaders? Is part of the problem the fact that we simply can't get our arms around anything that's whole because there isn't anything whole left anymore?

RIEBER: As Americans we are very easily manipulated, but with the coming of high technology we are becoming even more vulnerable to manipulation. The greater the social distress, the more likely people are to dissociate pressing social problems and forget them. They can be easily swept under the rug. And so people only pay attention to those fundamental problems that they have to deal with on an everyday basis in order to get through with their lives. So to the extent we dissociate, we are likely targets for the big sleep. Compare this situation to the Great Awakening, which was when this country was in its infancy and there were no mass media. And remember that the Great Awakening was the manipulation of the masses by preachers who gave them the gospel of their vision of the new society. Therefore, you have the Great Awakening on one end of the continuum and the great sleep on the other.

GIAMO: Is there any way to get out of this deep sleep? Do you see any new national purpose on the horizon?

RIEBER: Pay attention to the social dreams that we create and get in touch with their messages. They inform us of our unresolved problems. And one such dream is the message of Frankenstein. That's what we've created—a Frankenstein, and we are doing what was done to Frankenstein. We are not only Dr. Frankenstein but also the monster that he created. And yet we're not recognizing what we've done or why we've done it. The result is like the movie—the social dream—in which the masses are brainwashed into running after the monster of Frankenstein with their torches to kill him, killing the monster that is, as if killing the monster would take away the problem of his creation.

GIAMO: And leaving the inventor behind.

RIEBER: You can also see this form of social dissociation when you take into account how ordinary people reacted in Nazi Germany. This type of phenomenon (what Robert Jay Lifton calls numbing and doubling) takes place on both the individual and collective levels. I prefer to refer to this problem as social dissociation. So that's the kind of problem we are faced with. I'm afraid that the history of this country is one of brinksmanship, and we always push ourselves to the point where we're on the brink of a disaster until we wake up to face it. And then we keep reshuffling the cards and redefining the rules of the game, so that the closer we get to the brink the further we push it away. We're playing that game right now, so that we don't have to face what we really have in store for this generation. We can just give it to the next one. That's the way Washington operates and, as Washington goes, so goes the nation.

ROBERT COLES

The Human Context
of Homelessness

BENEDICT GIAMO: For over thirty years you have visited and worked with American children and their families from a variety of racial and ethnic backgrounds, across every social class, and from all regions of the country. And your purpose has been to work with children, to get to really know them over the long term—their hopes and dreams, sorrows, aspirations, struggles, feelings about self and identity, family and society. And in presenting these children's lives, you've often mentioned how much they've taught you. What do you feel these children and their families teach us about ourselves as individuals and as members of American society?

ROBERT COLES: Which children are you talking about?

GIAMO: Particularly the children from the poorer backgrounds and social conditions.

COLES: As you know, I try to avoid generalizations. I still ask which children because, frankly, I've worked with some children who were quite reticent and basically were not willing to have much to do with me or anyone else who wanted to talk with them. And, of course, those aren't the children I write about. The children I write about are those who are talkative or willing to become involved with me in a certain way so that I can learn from them. And that's an important caveat—to distinguish between a whole range of children and those particular children someone like me gets involved with.

I think poor children remind us about how lucky and fortunate we are who are not poor. If you spend enough time with poor children, you learn what troubles they have and how hard it can be for them. And presumably we'll realize, relatively speaking, how much easier it is for you or me as a fairly privileged person. Some children have taught me about the resiliency and inventiveness and ingenuity that's possible for those who are down-and-out, but nevertheless have their wits about them, and are able to contend with their difficult lives in a remarkable fashion. Conversely, other children remind me of how hard and tough it can be to be poor, and how broken people can become while living impoverished lives. Broken-hearted, broken in spirit, maybe even broken in a stricter psychiatric sense of becoming anxious and melancholy and disturbed, and even unable to organize the day for themselves in such a way that one lives coherently. Some people can be poor and tough and live hardscrabble but fiercely determined lives. Other people can be poor and be quite unable to make do.

GIAMO: In your writings, you seem to have drawn a distinction between the roles of the social observer and social critic. Time and time again you keep opting for a form of participant observation and description that goes along with fieldwork over and against a more abstract, generalized, and theoretical approach. How do you view the relationship between observer and critic?

COLES: It's *one* sensibility in my particular case. I don't draw the distinction. There's a part of me that observes, but there's also a part of me that tries to connect what I'm observing to the larger problems with our country or in the world. It's a seamless web, at least in my particular mind. I try not to speak in a categorical way—this moment as a social observer and that moment as a critic. I think this all is part of one's sensibility. At times one reaches out to people and tries to understand them, and at other times one pulls back a bit and maybe tries to connect that understanding to some sense of what is going on at large in the nation or the world.

GIAMO: But you often seem to caution against the excesses of critical theory.

COLES: Always. And to no avail that I've seen, at least every time I pick up a magazine or book.

GIAMO: It's getting more and more theoretical across all disciplines.

COLES: The social sciences value theory highly; it represents a means of their advancement. They're not in the business of valuing the wonderful insights of Raymond Carver or Tobias Wolff or Richard Ford, each of whom has an extraordinarily subtle and knowing view of troubled or down-and-out people, but who are not called social scientists. How lucky they are, I might add. Both not to be called that and not to be that.

G I A M O : It seems that you're carrying through with a more humanistic and traditional point of view in the way you approach your work and present it.

C O L E S : Well, that word "humanistic" has, of course, been appropriated by all sorts of people. And it's becoming another cliché, I regret to say.

G I A M O : By the way, when theorists want to criticize someone these days they call him or her a "humanist."

C O L E S : Really? Well that's how far out it has become with theorists. They don't even show an elementary respect for the value system that some others have.

G I A M O : "Modernism" is also a dirty word these days. And just now I saw a title in one of the Cambridge bookstores that claims we are in a phase of "late postmodernism." I mention this just in case you wanted to know where we are in terms of our time and place in the world.

C O L E S : Who cares about all these people? The abstract literary critics, the abstract social scientists! Who cares? As long as there's another Raymond Carver short story to read, or another novel by Tolstoy that one hasn't read and can now read, or read again, or another novel that's just come out by Richard Ford. I'll stay with that.

J E F F R E Y G R U N B E R G : Why is the importance of observable events often diminished by less available information? For instance, the inner turmoil of someone or the person's motive for doing something. It seems that the concrete is not given much credence and that what is at face value is often discarded.

C O L E S : Well, that's because we've spent 100 years valuing what isn't at face value to the point that it's become ironic if not absurd. The apparent gets dismissed while the hidden is rated as a great virtue to be sought. And that tells us more about ourselves than about the relative value of either the apparent or the concealed. Sometimes the most obvious things about people, which are very important in determining their lives, are brushed aside while investigators go ferreting out something else. I suppose it's our own sin of pride. We're trying to show what sleuths we are. And we are probably being rewarded for doing so by these universities.

GIAMO: Which we're a part of.

COLES: And many of which at times resemble a Ringling Brothers, Barnum and Bailey Circus. But you're not here to ask about that, I'm certain—the academic circus.

GRUNBERG: How did you decide on your own mission?

COLES: Honestly, I didn't *decide*. I fell into it by accident—all of which I've described in some of my books. I happened to be in the South at a particular time, saw what I saw, and became involved in it.

GRUNBERG: You left the emergency room?

COLES: Well, I left the conventional psychiatric and psychoanalytic practice that I would have had at the time.

GRUNBERG: Because of its penchant for the theoretical and categorical?

COLES: I never had any great interest in abstraction or theory. I majored in English, but not in the abstract English of literary criticism. I majored in English because I loved to read novels, short stories, and poems. I wrote my thesis on William Carlos Williams, who had no great love for the abstract. In fact, he was constantly decrying it in his poetry.

GIAMO: And Perry Miller, your tutor, was okay with that?

COLES: Perry Miller turned me on to Williams. And he was always ridiculing and laughing at abstract, big shot literary critics. As for the social sciences, he thought the whole enterprise was a joke. This goes way back, even to the early 1950s. So I come from this cranky tradition of skepticism with respect to high theory, be it of the social sciences or the humanities. And, by the way, to me high theory in the humanities is no more pleasing than high theory in the social sciences.

GIAMO: Is it fair to say that you start with life first, and not with the concept?

COLES: With the complexities, the ironies, the contradictions, the inconsistencies, which ought to be offered to oneself, accepted by oneself, and then restored and offered to others, if one happens to be in a position to do so.

GIAMO: That's interesting. It reminds me of another interview with you that was in *Times of Surrender*, a collection of your essays and reviews. In that particular interview you quoted Flannery O'Connor.

COLES: "The task of the novelist is not to 'resolve' mystery but to deepen it! And mystery is a great embarrassment to the modern mind." If O'Connor's remark isn't the rallying call, with respect to those of us who want to engage in this struggle with these theorists, whoever they might be—literary critics or social scientists—then I don't know what the rallying call is. To me, that is the rallying call.

GIAMO: So as a doctor-writer, do you try to do in your nonfiction what O'Connor attempted to do in her fiction?

COLES: Definitely. I regard myself as a storyteller. I listen to stories. I hear people tell me their stories. And I'm an intermediary between those people who tell the stories and those people who have some interest in reading them or hearing of them. Sometimes I tell the stories in a lecture and people listen to them, or I tell the stories as a writer.

GIAMO: And if an advocate or a reformer reads these stories, then says, "Hey, this fits in, this could inform social change"?

COLES: Well, if people want to do that, that's fine. But I've never fancied myself as a great political activist, although I did have a long period of involvement with the Civil Rights Movement. And I did work closely with Bobby Kennedy during the last couple years of his life when he was struggling with his own political direction, let alone with America's political direction.

GRUNBERG: Are you saying that you claim no goal?

COLES: No, I'm not saying that. It's a big goal to try to listen to people and listen to their stories.

GRUNBERG: I mean toward what end?

COLES: Well, I hope so that we'll all learn from one another and have a better-informed life.

GRUNBERG: So that people will learn from these stories?

COLES: Yes, to learn from these stories. To learn from these stories morally as well as intellectually, because a lot of these stories have, I think, some moral significance. And I think that I am trying to indicate that I respect these people enormously. That I regard them as teachers, not only as informants.

GRUNBERG: We all ought to look at them like that.

COLES: Well, the hope is that readers will be persuaded to. I can't go and grab the readers and shake them or compel them to do anything. But I think the underlying faith of a writer is that there's something of significance in what he or she is writing and that there will be some persuasiveness to this. I am not a deconstructionist; just the opposite. I believe that there can be a shared meaning in this life between two people—doctor and patient, husband and wife, parents and children. Shared meaning. And I think there is a shared meaning that writers can offer to readers, and that readers can jointly get from writers. So, to me, rampant, heady deconstructionism is just one more part of twentieth-century nihilism.

GIAMO: What is the basis of this shared meaning?

C O L E S: The basis of this shared meaning is our humanity and our common struggle to find meaning in life. That's what we're here for. We're the creature who has been given this gift of language, through whatever you call it—through biology, through psychology, through grace and God's wish. However you want to formulate it, we have language and we use this language to ask questions, to try to figure out the meaning of life. We ask questions such as Paul Gauguin wrote out when he did that triptych of his in 1897: "Where do we come from? What are we? Where are we going?"

G I A M O: The essential questions.

C O L E S: Yes, the essential questions. Even deconstructionists ask that. Even psychoanalysts who believe that those questions are merely Oedipal manifestations of a particular stage in child development. Even they ask them occasionally themselves.

G I A M O: When you strip all the rest of it away, that is what you are ultimately left with.

C O L E S: Ultimately, that is what you're left with—this knowing creature who uses words to try to understand himself or herself, and who reaches out to others, and who tries to figure out some sense of what this all really means in the brief time that each of us is allotted to do so.

G I A M O: I know you've identified George Orwell as one of your heroes.

C O L E S: I have a long list.

G I A M O: Do you feel, as Orwell did, that one of your major motivations has been to nudge the world in a certain direction?

C O L E S: Not only did Orwell feel that desire, but I think that's what all of the people I admire were trying to do: James Agee, Orwell, William Carlos Williams, Raymond Carver, Walker Percy, Flannery O'Connor, Ralph Ellison, Zora Neale Hurston, and the great Victorian writers— George Eliot, Thomas Hardy, Charles Dickens, or in Russia Tolstoy and

Dostoevsky. In some way they were trying to share a vision with the reader and hoped that the reader would thereby be affected. Maybe affected is less pushy than influenced.

G I A M O : But you don't seem to get preoccupied with discerning to what extent the world is responding to the way you want to nudge it.

C O L E S : No, no. And I think it's important to emphasize that I did not go South during the Civil Rights Movement. I went South to go into the doctor's draft and to be in charge of a psychiatric hospital in Mississippi before the Civil Rights Movement started. I happened to be in the South. I basically came from a nonpolitical tradition. My father was a Republican who admired Robert Taft. My mother, in a rather desultory sort of way, voted Democratic. I was not a highly political person when I started this work. And although I had formed a strong friendship, I think it's fair to say, with Robert Kennedy, and was very close to Dr. Martin Luther King in the early 1960s when we used to go to the Southern Regional Council meetings, and although I worked with Bob Moses, and was in the Mississippi Summer Project, and was very much involved with the whole Civil Rights Movement—with all that, I still say that I don't sign a lot of petitions, and I don't get all involved in politics. Sometimes I'm as skeptical of a lot of liberals and political radicals as I am of conservatives. Sometimes even more so, because it's incumbent upon one to want to be skeptical of one's own kind. And I find at times liberal intellectuals are as capable of arrogance and smugness and self-importance as any conservatives I've met in this country or abroad, maybe more so.

G I A M O : Well, you know, that's part of the reason for this collection of interviews—to present a more complete understanding of homelessness. Many of the advocates are oversimplifying the nature of the social problem and, as a result, misstating it.

C O L E S : They sure are. They sure are. Some insist it's housing, housing, housing. And it's the homeless as a kind of normal population that has been desperately taken advantage of by a cruel economic system. And I think that's a simplification.

G I A M O : The sledgehammer of dispossession?

C O L E S : That's right. At times it's become political rhetoric, I regret to say. I know, I've talked with homeless people I think are frankly psychotic in a severe sense of the word—extremely disturbed and incoherent. And I don't feel that as a human being, never mind as a psychiatrist, I shouldn't acknowledge that as part of their problem and part of our problem as society. By the way, I did a review of two recent books that came out on homelessness. One of them was quite "conservative." And because I simply responded and said, "Look, some of this is true and important to be stated," I started getting hell from the people who read the review.

G I A M O : You seem to have a lot of balance in your work.

C O L E S : I don't know whether I have balance, or whether I'm just cranky. I got into trouble with some of the nuclear activists for not joining in with the way they described children as being abused and panicked and frightened by the fear that the nuclear holocaust was around the corner. I've been talking to these children for years, all sorts of children, and I don't hear it from them. And I asked them, I made a point of asking them, and asking them. And they [the children] began to look at me as if I was in trouble.

G R U N B E R G : I think, in part, you're getting at something that often bothers me about how people approach working with the homeless.

C O L E S : Quote "the homeless." "The homeless" are a whole potpourri of individuals, some of whom don't have any money and are sane and solid and need some money. Some of them have some money but not enough to pay for rent in a city that just doesn't have available housing for them. Some of them are out-and-out alcoholics and psychotics, or down-and-out people who in the old days used to be in the Bowery or in places here on Beacon Hill that we had where they could find some kind of community. And now we've gentrified these places.

G R U N B E R G : We've often said that homelessness has become truly homeless since the early 1980s. The Bowery, for instance, has disappeared as a skid row neighborhood.

COLES: True, the Bowery has disappeared. And these places in the back of Beacon Hill, where Boston's skid row was located, have disappeared. So all of that has gone. And, of course, as a result, we have homelessness. But to lump homelessness into one problem, and then to wail at the country indiscriminately as being callous and indifferent to the homeless, I just don't think is fair—either to the "homeless" or to this nation.

GRUNBERG: In so many social service programs, professionals automatically say that people who are homeless are vulnerable and weak, frightened, and in need of protection. And when I'm talking to them I see the opposite. I see a vibrant, heterogeneous group. Some of whom are not lazy. Some of whom are hilarious and extremely bright.

COLES: And some of whom are mean-spirited and nasty, outrageously difficult human beings.

GRUNBERG: You're blaming the victim now. (laughter) You realize that, and that's what you'll be accused of. You're blaming the victim. (laughter)

COLES: Listen, in recent years I've been accused of a number of things. So I'm not afraid to have this accusation too. (laughter) When I listened to Helen Caldicott talking about ten years ago I thought: I don't know which is worse, a nuclear bomb or the crazy talk that she was coming out with. She was going on and on about what would happen with Reagan as president, and how the whole world was going to come to an end, and she was screaming and screeching at children and in junior high schools and high schools. And, meanwhile, where are we after eight years of Reagan? Listen to what was said and predicted by her and others, and look at where we are now, and you'll see that craziness is not just a function of the so-called right. Or, by the way, of psychotically homeless people! Craziness can also be on the left, from prominent, well-respected people on the left. So I think it behooves some of us to be self-critical before we launch an assault on others we claim to disagree with.

GIAMO: What do you see as the primary issues involved in homelessness?

COLES: There are some people who have a rough time in this society, for various reasons. And some of those people who have a rough time end up on the street. There is no asylum where they can be hospitalized. There is no community they can turn to, such as the old skid row community, the Bowery. There are apartments, but they cost $1,000 a month. Or some of the homeless have a personality that doesn't enable them to save money, enough to use to put a deposit down.

I talked with a homeless family in a church in Cambridge. This was a white, Irish homeless family. This was a mother who was not an alcoholic, who was not psychotic. She did have a job and a fairly good job. But there was some disorganization in her and she spent her money in such a way that she never had quite enough so that she could find an apartment and put down a deposit on it. And when I questioned her closely, I thought to myself: I could find a home for her if I had control over her income. I'd help her to save and teach her the importance of putting away some money so that she could make that deposit, and so that she would find this more important than some of the things she was spending money on. Okay, maybe I'm begging the question. Maybe she's literally "psychiatrically disturbed," although not psychotic to the point that she needs help. And she does need some help from me. But I'm trying to point out that here's someone who defied the usual categories of psychosis, of drug addiction and alcoholism. And for that matter, of living in a society that has no apartments because of gentrification. There *were* apartments. I thought they were fairly reasonable compared to her income. But she had no willingness or determination or whatever to organize her income in such a way that she was able to pay the rent. Now, okay, I explored this and realized that she was depressed. Well, what else am I going to come up with? Some part of me, of course, is going to come up with the fact that she's depressed.

GIAMO: Children in the family?

COLES: Three children.

G I A M O : And what did the children tell you? Did you have them do pictures?

C O L E S : I did.

G I A M O : What did they tell you through these pictures?

C O L E S : Well, they drew pictures of houses that they had seen. And they told me that this is where they'd like to live. Then I asked them to draw a picture of their mother. And two of them would not. And the third, when he finished drawing the picture of his mother (especially by the way he drew her hair and her face), said to me without a word basically what I had already concluded. Since I've had some experience with children who draw pictures of their parents over the last three decades, I thought he was telling me that his mother was disorganized and downcast. Not crazy, but disorganized and downcast. The eyes were down. The ears were curved in such a way that she couldn't really hear. Of course, this is me interpreting the child's drawing. But he also told me what the problem was.

G R U N B E R G : This is very exciting for me to hear because I've been working with the homeless in a hands-on kind of way for about nine years. And I have always said, "Bring to me any homeless person and I will show you how he or she can not be homeless in a matter of months." They will have to become protagonists. But given his or her abilities, whether mentally ill or not, there's a way to tap resources. Because they need help, especially in organizing and redirecting their lives. Not case management, necessarily, because often that involves infantilizing them.

C O L E S : Infantilization is something that has been close to the heart of all too many of us middle-class liberals who love various groups to be somehow in a dependent relationship to us, whether it be politically, or socioeconomically, or culturally, or whatever. We love to patronize various others, I'm afraid to say. Of course, we don't acknowledge this—say it in magazines. (laughter) This is the problem, you see. You *say* these things and the political right picks it up!!

G I A M O: And they use it as ammunition.

C O L E S: Right.

G I A M O: Well, I guess that's a necessary risk of a project like this which attempts to get beyond rigid ideological classifications—whether from the political right or from the political left. Both the right and left seem to sidetrack the public from the *whole* social conflict. The real issues that need to be confronted are somehow displaced, cast aside.

C O L E S: Well, you're not here to talk about this, but one of the issues with children is relevant to what we're just talking about. Now the liberals are always saying, "Let's give these kids condoms in the ghettos." But they would never give their own children condoms.

G R U N B E R G: Or clean needles.

C O L E S: Or clean needles. They'd never give their own kids clean needles or condoms. Basically, what they're saying is that *we* write *them* off. Just get *them* out of the way. Stop *them* from propagating.

G R U N B E R G: Or infecting us.

C O L E S: Or infecting us. Just get rid of them. What these kids need, by the way, is moral and spiritual and psychological help. They need better . . .

G R U N B E R G: Opportunities?

C O L E S: Yes, but they also need a stronger family. They need a moral life. They need something to believe in. And in that sense, the churches are absolutely right. They need constraints and controls. Psychoanalysis and the Catholic church actually come together on this. They need psychological development, moral development, family strengthening. And how are we going to do that? To throw condoms at them is basically saying, "We don't give a God damn about your sexuality. Go ahead and do it."

GRUNBERG: So the right and the left end up doing something similar.

COLES: Definitely.

GIAMO: And where's the basis for the shared meaning you talked about earlier?

COLES: That's the way, I'm afraid, on both the right and the left, that this is being looked at. Less so, I think, on the right, actually, than on the left, because of the religious side of the right. For crying out loud, there has to be some constraint and control in the lives of these people. And how do we do it? The right says they don't care how, but they're willing to say it's needed. The left says, "Hey, that's not the way we're even going to look at the problem."

GRUNBERG: Unfortunately, when the left talks, the right reacts and then you get into a dynamic in which everyone is misstating the problem. They're reacting almost solely to each other. "Wait in the hallway; we're busy in here." How then does one become politically responsible, and yet true to oneself and what one sees as an individual?

COLES: You say what you believe in, on the basis of what you've seen and heard.

GIAMO: Whether it smacks of the right or smacks of the left, or beyond the right or left, or what have you?

COLES: That's what I believe. When I start censoring what I've heard and seen from children in order to tailor it to a particular ideology or point of view of colleagues in Cambridge, or New Haven, or New York, I'm through. Then, in my opinion, I should stop this work.

GIAMO: Because for you it's a moral position to take, to be true . . .

COLES: To what I've heard and seen. If children are not telling me that the world is going to blow up due to a nuclear bomb, I'm not going to say that they are telling me that in order to please some friends in the

Northeast who are called liberal intellectuals, or whatever they're called. And by the same token, if I meet a homeless person who is not psychotic and not alcoholic, but sort of disorganized, and frankly, morally irresponsible, I think it's my job to say that. Not to make a generalization and say that all homeless people are morally irresponsible, but to tell the truth that I met this person, talked with her for a few days, and found out that basically she's a helter-skelter scatterbrain who definitely needs to be tethered to a kind of reality which she doesn't have functioning for her because of the effects of this kind of behavior on her children and on herself. But I can't call her psychotic and I can't call her an alcoholic and I can't call her a victim of this society. She has a job. She just takes that money and spends it, I think, irresponsibly. And what am I supposed to do then? Call her a victim of a cruel capitalistic system? Say that she's totally out of her mind and needs to be in a mental hospital? Say that she's drinking too much or shooting up drugs? None of that is true.

Now, you may say there aren't too many people like her. Well, I've met a few. I've met a few. And then I've met some [homeless] people whom I used to call, as a psychiatrist, hopeless, down-and-out alcoholics. When I was a resident at Massachusetts General in the Alcoholism Clinic, they used to live in so-called flophouses in Boston. And we were lucky to have those places for those people. And now that we've gotten rid of them, we do have a problem as to where they're going to stay. But let's not suddenly turn the lives of those, mostly men, as I knew them in the 1950s, into an excuse for a political jeremiad. Let's not call this country a cruel one that neglects the innocent. We have a complicated problem here!

GRUNBERG: Well, let's not give our parks away, and let's not give away all public spaces.

COLES: That's right. And let's realize that sometimes those people can take our parks, and our banks, and our stores, and the streets and turn them into a mayhem—assaulting people, intruding on their lives, making life miserable for others. And those other people have some rights too. They're ordinary citizens. They're going to work. They're trying to enjoy public space.

Well, you know, I should say something really important in my own work that I think conditions me along these lines. I have spent years talking to so-called working-class people. They work in factories. They're blue-collar workers. They work in offices, as so-called white-collar workers. They work very hard. Some of them have two jobs, even three jobs, to try to get by. These are people who are not exploiting anyone. If anything, they're being exploited, I suppose, because sometimes they only get about four or five hours' sleep. Hard, hard-working people who have learned to be thrifty, who have learned to be careful, who have learned not to indulge themselves and overindulge themselves. Who have learned even, sometimes, to save a few dollars for their kids. And when those people are told by people like me (who are, relatively speaking, well off and comfortable) that in some way they're hard of heart and callous and mean-spirited because their impulse, when they see some homeless people, is to say, "For crying out loud, give us a break." Or, "Go to work and get a job." (There *are* some jobs available.) Then I find this very, very challenging to me morally. Very challenging. And I'm trying to put myself in the shoes of a lot of people who are "different." Well, I think I should try to put myself in the shoes of those [working-class] people too. And I shouldn't just patronize those people and say that they're insensitive, reactionary, and callous, and all these other words that some people, like me, use with respect to those who have a few doubts about some of the things that are going on in this country. And among them, at least some aspects of the so-called problem of homelessness. *Some* aspects.

GIAMO: All of this must have come to the surface during the busing crisis here in Boston.

COLES: You bet. Read Tony Lukas' book, *Common Ground*. I had a run-in with liberals here in Boston back then. I said the working-class people are being asked to desegregate their schools. But the rich buy their way out of the city. Even after they've done that, they buy their way out of the affluent suburban public schools with private schools. And no one has ever asked them to do anything, and no one was calling them racist and prejudiced people. They buy their way out of that too. So you can buy your way out of anything. And people were being dumped on and being criticized and called racists and rednecks. Who were they? They're vulnerable too. They're vulnerable, working-class people, an easy prey for the liberal characterizations of people like me who have never been tested in our lives the way a lot of people have been tested by various federal court orders. Never been tested, and always slipping out of this through the schools we send our kids to, the privileges we have, and the neighborhoods we're able to live in. And then we have the ultimate privilege—we use fancy language, psychiatric, psychological, and sociological, to put down all the people we disagree with. Then there is the ultimate privilege beyond that—that the newspapers, the liberal papers, pay a lot of attention to us. That's a nice deal.

GRUNBERG: Let's stay on that for a little while. I wanted to ask you a few questions about the rich and the poor. Do you think they see each other as outsiders? What would happen if they intermingled? Would anything change as a result, if they really got to know each other?

COLES: Well, I think it's going to be a hard thing to bring about. I don't see any hope of it being realized. In my work with some very wealthy families, I find that some of them are as cut off from the reality of the world as the poor. They're as cut off from the social and economic reality of life as the poor are. As I've described in some of my writing, the rich and very well off live within secluded, protected environments that have a stunning unreality to them. And many of them know very little about money or work. And their children know even less. The children have been, in their own way, "disadvantaged" by this kind of surreal world that they've either inherited or that someone in the family has enabled them to have. Then, having enabled them to have that, they don't have much else other than that. So they're cut off. And this is a supreme irony.

The people who are in intimate contact with all life's contingencies, social and economic, whatever, are the ordinary working people who each day have to go out there and try to get through that day. Dealing with clocks that they check in with, and clocks that they check out with. And dealing with bosses, dealing with the stock market reality as it affects the likelihood that they may be fired. Always dealing with the consequences of recession. Not the way we deal with it by reading about it in the *New York Times* and wondering about it, but by losing their jobs. People like me who are working in universities and have "tenure" don't lose our jobs. And this gives us our own little air of unreality at times as we contemplate the world. We stress Oedipus complexes, and we stress one or another aspect of the world, like the nuclear bomb as a distinct danger, or the environment as a danger. But we don't have to face that everyday possibility of just losing our jobs and being out there without a penny and collecting from unemployment. So what are our priorities that matter? And how do those priorities tell us about our particular lives? And, therefore, what kind of parochialism, insularity, and callousness are *we* capable of?

GRUNBERG: I guess social distance between classes is inevitable.

COLES: Not necessarily. At the risk of romanticization, as Tolstoy reminded us, sometimes landowners and the people who work for them get close. Sometimes, even in the worst of the South, white people and black people knew one another a lot better than white people and black people do up North. In fact, I'll never forget Bob Moses getting the Mississippi Summer Project going. He reminded us—these well-meaning and fine northern college students going to go into Mississippi in the summer of 1964—that in the South the black and white people had a kind of intimacy that was distinctly lacking up North. This is not to condone segregation or to undercut the need for that whole Civil Rights struggle, but just to give pause to some of us abstract, vociferous liberals who can denounce, at a distance, inequities and injustices in other parts of the country or world. And who are never really tested in our ordinary lives about how we live. What do we know? What kind of knowledge do we have of black people or Spanish-speaking people?

GRUNBERG: The race issue: with black homeless people outnumbering white homeless people, as much as 7 to 1 in some cities, can't one consider homelessness here in the twentieth century merely a contemporary version of a historical condition of homelessness, perhaps 300 years of it? Is homelessness then, in part, a result of racism?

COLES: Well, you always ask *which* black homeless, and why are they homeless? I mean, what is the problem? Joblessness? Personal anarchy? Drug addiction? Disintegration of moral and psychological life? You just have to ask which. It won't do just to quote the figures. Let us get beyond the statistics to the individual instances and try to learn what those instances collectively have to tell us. If 1,000 blacks are homeless, and 950 of them are homeless because drug addiction has taken away their reasonable capacity for work and for a fighting chance to make do in this world, then I think we've got to put that on the table honestly and recognize it as a problem. Don't simply say that it's a racist society. I just don't think that's right.

GRUNBERG: Where is the place for intention? For example, if society knows that drugs are a problem, but says, "So what? That's their problem." Hazel Dukes spoke of the "conspiracy of silence" that white and black leaders are both subject to.

COLES: A silence about what?

GRUNBERG: About the fact that the numbers are so disproportionate that maybe this is going on and on and on because those affected are black. The victims are black. So perhaps there is, as a result, less concern that we ought to do something about the problem.

COLES: I don't know whether that's true or not. I mean it was quite possible in this society historically for well-to-do, well-educated people to be utterly indifferent toward lots and lots of *white* people, for generations of them: the Irish in Boston, or the immigrants in New York who came to this country in the early part of the century and lived under abominable circumstances, or lots of people today in Appalachia who are white, who are coal miners, or who are trying to live hardscrabble lives off the land. There is utter indifference on the part of society toward them. That's not racism. It's just indifference, terrible indifference. Class based, I suppose you'd call it. Class is just as important as race. And, sometimes, what we call race is really class. But it's called race because of race, which may be an ultimate form of racism, in which we racistly confuse the class problem with the race problem. I'm not saying it always happens.

I mean, after all, there are lots of black people who are strong and resilient and resourceful and have worked their way up from poverty, and they have done damn good jobs of it, of doing it themselves. Let us acknowledge that achievement and that possibility. And if it's a possibility that isn't seized upon by many people, let's find out why, and let's be honest about it. Why? Why in this case? Why in that case? Then look at all the evidence and describe what we've heard and seen, and then go from there. But if I'm going to simply say it's all racism, then I don't think I'm doing justice to human particularity. The homeless and all the rest of the people on God's earth deserve their individuality.

GRUNBERG: Is affirmative action then also begging the point?

COLES: At times it can. I'm not saying it always does. I think there may be instances of utter inequity based on hate and meanness and prejudice that we have to assault, in whatever way we can, and take on. But if a person is told that because he or she is black, or speaks Spanish, or is Asian American, or Native American then you're automatically a victim of prejudice and that should be your faith, and that's *the* way society judges you, then I think that is the ultimate kind of prejudice directed at the person.

GRUNBERG: The last thing you want is for people to limit themselves that way.

COLES: Or to feel that society has limited them in that categorical way.

GRUNBERG: So even if color is an issue, and the minute I walk into the room you're going to notice I'm black and hold certain ideas about me, I should think that we're all holding ideas about each other.

COLES: There have to be contacts. When I hear from people that men can't understand women, and whites can't understand blacks, and people who don't speak Spanish can't understand people who do speak Spanish, I'm reminded that there has to be a human context to this. Half of American marriages end up in divorce. These are husbands and wives of presumably the same social background. And there's an enormous amount of misunderstanding between parents and children. That's why James Agee started out *Let Us Now Praise Famous Men* with a selection from *King Lear*. It was to remind us that, if you're going to have trouble, as Agee did, understanding sharecroppers in Alabama in 1936 because of class, educational, and cultural disparities, there was once a father, Lear, and his daughters, and *they* all had a hell of a lot of trouble understanding themselves. And there weren't class disparities among *them*. This is the important context we all have to remind ourselves of.

GIAMO: Would you say there are systemic flaws as well as tragic flaws?

COLES: Yes, there are both systemic and tragic flaws. There are social inequities and historical injustices. And there is plenty of racism and mean-spiritedness, and hatred and bigotry. I've spent my life documenting them. I don't feel I have to repeat that *per se*. But I do feel it's important for you to hear from someone like me that beyond all that are individuals who I think ought to be accorded the respect of particular documentary scrutiny—the respect offered by those of us who are claiming to do justice to their situation. And I think all efforts to subsume people under various categorizations ought to be regarded skeptically.

GIAMO: Once again, start with life.

COLES: Start with individual human variation and particularity and see where it leads us to. If I start that way and I start hearing that the only problem, say, with homelessness is that there aren't enough houses, and if that goes against what I've experienced in my particular involvement with homeless people, then I say this is a political cliché or a sociological cliché or some kind of cliché. I say cliché because it doesn't fit with what I've seen and felt and heard and understood. Generalization may be the word rather than cliché.

GRUNBERG: What role do you think chance plays in the development of crisis?

COLES: Chance plays a role in everyone's life, a big role. Sometimes people end up homeless because their husbands walked out on them. They left not because they [the wives] were alcoholics or mean-spirited or psychotic. Maybe they met someone that they liked better, and they fell in love. You're left with a novel here. And the husbands left behind a saddened, perplexed family. Well, in a way that's chance. Historically, it's also chance when a developer comes in and starts tearing down what is, in its own way, a tight-knit community of people. That's chance. Chance is a part of all of our lives. Sometimes chance works very positively. Perhaps someone who is vulnerable or troubled meets a particular person and helps that person enormously, and becomes a rescuer—morally, psychologically, spiritually. I wouldn't be sitting and talking with you right now if I hadn't by chance stumbled into my wife. It was a total fluke and an accident. And if I hadn't been married to her, believe me, I wouldn't have done this kind of work. Because, in various ways, she encouraged and affirmed this work as important when I was ready to walk away from it. So that's chance.

GRUNBERG: Looking at things that way, it sounds like you put a great amount of emphasis on personal responsibility when working with people.

COLES: What else is there, if it's not personal responsibility? And who am I to take it away as a desirable thing from anyone? And who am I to condescend and patronize people by saying they are totally helpless, and the only thing that will get them by is me and my kind and our programs? Personal responsibility is our last chance in this life.

GRUNBERG: So then there's nothing wrong with the "bootstrap" approach?

COLES: I don't see anything wrong with encouraging people to open whatever doors they possibly can by working very hard, by working very hard. Even to the point that there is pain in that work. When I was a teenager, my father insisted that I work, and told me I had to work. And I remember spending a whole summer working in a laundry in a hospital in Boston. All the soiled linen came pouring down on me. And when I picked all that soiled linen up, I took it over to the hottest God damn room in the hospital where the machines were, and where the laundry was being put in. They gave us salt pills because we were sweating so hard during the day working in that room. I'm not saying I enjoyed that work. I was underpaid. I didn't get the amount of money that I felt I should get. I know there were a lot of people doing less difficult work that were being paid more. But somehow I got through that spell. And it meant something to me to be able to do that. And I think I learned something about myself and other people. And I made some money, and I saved it. And I think this kind of experience is not beyond other people too.

GRUNBERG: It's almost as if the most pragmatic way one can look at the homeless is seeing them as a new kind of immigrant or internal alien. "You've had a lot of problems. You're dirt poor, in dire straits. But you're in America; you've made it, that is, you've survived. Now you're here. You don't have a place to live yet, but take it from here."

COLES: Let's take it from here. Let's find what we can do and where we can be and where we can live.

GIAMO: Social perceptions often determine what we see, comprehend (morally and spiritually as well as intellectually), and, ultimately, what we do about social problems, be they poverty or homelessness. During a conversation with Daniel Berrigan (in *The Geography of Faith*), you asked: "What is it that people don't want to see about the world around them, and why?" At present, how would you come to terms with that same question? Is it still a question that you ask yourself today?

COLES: Yes. I arraign myself at times. What is it that I am failing to see about people? What is it that makes me want to stress, maybe, environmental concerns or nuclear warfare concerns when, in fact, the concerns of the people that I'm talking about have nothing to do with either environmental concerns or nuclear warfare concerns, but have to do with bread and butter concerns. "Will I hold onto this job?" "Will my kid get a fairly decent education in this school, when someone wants to send them to another school that I'm scared out of my mind for the kid to go to?" I mean, those are the ordinary concerns that I hear from the people I work with in working-class neighborhoods throughout Boston and in Framingham and Worcester (in Massachusetts). So I have to ask myself not only what prejudices do they have (what blind spots, what failures in vision), but what about *me*? What in my life has made me insensitive to certain people, and all too sensitive to other people. So there's a disparity there too—one that tells you a lot about my hangups and difficulties and parochialism. I'm part of the problem.

GIAMO: You've always included yourself as a part of your observations and reflections.

COLES: Of course! And all these so-called social scientists and observers and writers, they're part of this "reality," this social and political reality, too.

GRUNBERG: They try to stay out of it. People try to stay out of it.

COLES: We're a part of this. What have we failed to see? Why are we espousing this particular line of inquiry or that particular program? And what does that tell us about ourselves—never mind about the problems we're presuming to say we're interested in, the problems we want to solve more "radically"?

GIAMO: So, really, there is no exit out of asking these types of questions into human nature and the moral imagination.

COLES: No exit is the phrase. That's what Sartre said. There is "no exit."

GIAMO: But your view, it seems, is that if we all make ourselves more aware personally and individually we will improve the common good.

COLES: I think we'll improve our knowledge of one another, which is supposedly my job anyway, to try to do that first of all with myself and then with readers. We'll know more candidly about one another.

GIAMO: You would also like to alleviate the suffering, if you do see and experience such suffering?

COLES: Of course. Of course. Of course. But I don't want to alleviate suffering in such a way that I am callous and cruelly indifferent to the truth, to the troubles of one set of people while emphasizing the troubles of another. I think I have to be as honest as I possibly can, across the board. And then let's start in doing the best we can to reach out to one another. How can I help people if I don't really understand what their difficulties are? How can I say to the woman, whom I keep mentioning to you, that her difficulty is there aren't enough apartments, when I know in my heart of hearts that that isn't the difficulty? Rather, there is a personal difficulty in her mind that prevents her from taking advantage of the ordinary resources she, in fact, has already. I would not be helping that woman one bit by this kind of political rhetoric which ignores her condition. I don't mean to be cruel or indifferent to her. I don't think she stands alone. I think there are others like her. She needs medical or, rather, psychiatric help.

GRUNBERG: Do you feel, as you're moving through your years, that America is now at a point where there are more people with these sorts of difficulties, personal problems, or whatever, than ever before? Or is it just that people with such problems are more visible now?

COLES: I don't know the answer to that. I just don't know.

GRUNBERG: You don't sense America going down the tubes?

COLES: No, I don't. Listen, I worked in the emergency ward at Massachusetts General Hospital in the late 1950s when people came to us with all kinds of difficulties. And a lot of them, we sent right back to the flophouses where they came from. We were able to get some women to mental hospitals. We had certain resources available that are not available now. I'm not saying that even if those resources were available, there still wouldn't be very serious problems with homelessness, problems having to do with what we all hear about: namely, gentrification, unemployment, and inadequate social and economic resources on the part of certain populations; but it is important to emphasize that there is a whole range of difficulties here encompassed by that word "homelessness," as I keep repeating.

GIAMO: You always seem to unravel what "the cloistered weaver" has spun. In a sense, you seem to yank away at those all too facile social conceptions, those neatly woven theories, those "supreme fictions," to borrow a phrase from Wallace Stevens, and remind us of the context—encounter, observation, description—in which we may begin again, perhaps reweaving with new threads.

COLES: Well, thank you for putting it that way. But the skeptic would say that you're setting me up in a nice way. I would prefer to think that I am not trying to unravel anything that anyone has woven. All I'm trying to do, phenomenologically, is observe and record as honestly and searchingly and forthrightly as I know how—allowing for my blind spots, inadequacies, failures of vision, hangups . . .

GIAMO: Your humanity.

COLES: My humanity. That's it, you got it.

We—the "symbol-using, symbol-misusing animal," as Kenneth Burke reminds us—are both blessed and cursed by the peculiar gift of language, by intellectual conception and emotional expression, by the unique ability to relate experiences in terms that round up the chaos of the world into patterned frames of reference. Language, thought, perception, and attitude: these are the qualities that set us in motion and keep the dance alive, pressing on, generation after generation. Admittedly, at times the dance is reminiscent of the playful and bewildering antics of a monkey house; but, at other times, it becomes an imperfect circle, like Henri Matisse's painting, where two hands reaching out for completion in the rounded swirl of dancers make all the difference.

This book has been a collection of such dances (call them interviews) on contemporary homelessness that attempts to prod American society out of the monkey house of social conception. Having said that, we must add: who among us, those of us who have stepped into these interviews, has not had that not all so aboriginal urge to scratch and leap and banter about with his or her own versions of the "social problem"? In other words, we (investigators and citizens alike) *are* an inescapable part of all that constitutes the social problem, and the problems of the homeless are integral to the conditions of social life in America and the human drama that each of us, in his or her own way, is captured by.

This recognition is necessary to the purpose of this book, which aims to reclaim a deeper understanding of the complex dimensions that comprise the conditions of homelessness in America. The public response is also viewed as part and parcel of such conditions. During his interview, Robert Coles inadvertently spoke to the significance of this collection while commenting on more essential human matters: "Ultimately, that is what you're left with—this knowing creature who uses words to try to understand himself or herself, and who reaches out to others, and who tries to figure out some sense of what this all really means in the brief time that each of us is allotted to do so." Put into the context of this project, we (both interviewers and interviewees) are precisely those "creatures" who yearn to question, to comprehend, to know, and then, in reaching beyond these moments of discourse, to tell others who might care to join the dance.

NOTES ON CONTRIBUTORS

ROBERT COLES, winner of the Pulitzer Prize in 1973 for volumes 2 and 3 of his *Children of Crisis* series, is often described as one of the leading authorities on the issues of poverty and racial discrimination in America. He has written numerous books on such topics as drug abuse, impoverished children and families, women in crisis, and education. His most recent publication, *The Spiritual Life of Children*, followed other books which focused on the moral and political development of children and their resilience in the face of poverty and extreme adversity. Coles has extended his research and writing to other aspects of social psychiatry, biography, and literary studies. He has written books on James Agee, Dorothy Day, Erik Erikson, Flannery O'Connor, Walker Percy, Simone Weil, and William Carlos Williams. Currently a Distinguished Professor of Psychiatry at Harvard University, Dr. Coles is a physician, teacher, writer, and activist.

HAZEL DUKES is president of both the National Association for the Advancement of Colored People (NAACP) and its New York State Conference, as well as executive director of the New York City's Off-Track Betting Corporation's Logistic Services. She has worked most of her life as a community organizer, rallying social support and action for interracial justice. Since receiving her bachelor's degree from Alabama State Technical College and her master's degree from Adelphi University, she has served on the Board of the Town of Hempstead's Urban Renewal Program and the Nassau Commission's Board of Consumer Affairs. Dukes was also a Carter appointee to the National Council on Economic Opportunity. She has received numerous awards for her activism and community service, including the Guardian "Person of the Year" Award (1979) and the Catholic Interracial Council of New York's John Lafarge Memorial Award for Interracial Justice (1980).

JAMES R. DUMPSON, twice the former commissioner of New York City's Department of Social Welfare and former dean of Fordham University's Graduate School of Social Service, has convened several mayoral panels studying a variety of social problems. *A Shelter Is Not a Home*, which investigated causes and solutions related to family homelessness, was the result of one such study commissioned by then Manhattan borough president David Dinkins. Dr. Dumpson has written several books, including *Evaluation of Social Intervention* (1972) and *Beyond Civil Rights: The Right to Economic Security* (1976). He currently serves as chairman of the Health and Hospitals Corporation and as senior consultant to both the New York Community Trust and the Welfare Research Institute.

BENEDICT GIAMO received his M.A. in psychology from the Graduate Faculty of the New School for Social Research and his Ph.D. in American Studies from Emory University. He has been working with and studying the condition of the homeless for the past fifteen years. His recent book *On the Bowery: Confronting Homelessness in America* approaches the enduring problem of homelessness from an interdisciplinary perspective, combining historical and literary studies with contemporary fieldwork. He was awarded the 1988 Ralph Henry Gabriel Prize of the American Studies Association for this work. He has also written articles on the relationship of homelessness to the broader context of poverty and affluence in American society. Currently, he is an assistant professor of American Studies at the University of Notre Dame.

JEFFREY GRUNBERG received his M.A. in psychology from the Graduate Faculty of the New School for Social Research and was trained in family therapy at the Institute for Mental Health. He has been involved in research on the homeless along with program design, development, and delivery throughout New York City for the past fifteen years. He holds an appointment as an associate professor of clinical psychology at Columbia University and is vice-president of social services for the Grand Central and 34th Street Partnerships, nonprofit organizations serving the homelsss in midtown Manhattan. He has written a variety of articles on the homeless situation and serves on the advisory board for the *Journal of Social Distress and the Homeless*.

The late JERZY KOSINSKI was a novelist whose survivalist morality, coupled with explicit scenes of violence and sex in his books, made him a controversial figure. Born in 1933 in Lodz, Poland, Kosinski came to the United States in 1957. He drew on his own experiences as a Jewish child in Poland during World War II to write *The Painted Bird*, a novel about a six-year-old boy who, separated from his parents, wanders homeless around Eastern Europe and witnesses the horrors of war. Kosinski received the National Book Award in 1969 for *Steps*, a book that deals with the pain of adjustment to American society. He also received the American Academy of Arts and Letters Award for Literature in 1970 and the American Civil Liberties Union First Amendment Award in 1978. Throughout his shortened career, in which he produced nine novels, two works of nonfiction, and numerous essays and articles, Kosinski was concerned with individualism, the rigors of adaptation in the face of repression, and creative problem-solving.

ROBERT JAY LIFTON, former professor of psychiatry at Yale University, is currently a Distinguished Professor at the City University of New York. The bulk of Dr. Lifton's research has been on the psychologies of the victims and survivors of historical tragedies, such as the Holocaust, the bombing of Hiroshima, and the Vietnam War. He has also investigated the psychologies of the perpetrators of such victimization and the relationship between death imagery and violence. His most recent work, *The Genocidal Mentality: Nazi Holocaust and Nuclear Threat* (1990), examines the psychological methods people use to suspend normal morality. Lifton's awards include the National Book Award for Science in 1969 for *Death in Life: Survivors of Hiroshima*, the National Jewish Book Award for *The Nazi Doctors* (1986), and the Gandhi Peace Award in 1984. Dr. Lifton has been an active supporter of nuclear disarmament and civil rights. He has also produced two collections of cartoons, *Birds* and *Psycho Birds*.

MARY ROSE MCGEADY, a member of the Daughters of Charity, has spent most of her life helping destitute children, the homeless, and the mentally ill. Formerly a staff member of the Homes of Destitute Catholic Children and regional director of Catholic Charities in Boston, Sister McGeady presently serves as the executive director of Covenant House, which serves about 1,500 youths every night in eight locations across the country. In this position, she has helped the organization to renew its commitment to helping homeless children and adolescents, expand its services, and reach out to the public in order to educate and gain support. Sister McGeady has also written *God's Lost Children*, a testimonial of her experiences with the youth with whom she works.

HERBERT PARDES is currently serving as the chairman of Columbia Presbyterian Medical Center's Department of Psychiatry and vice-president for health sciences at Columbia University. Formerly the president of the American Psychiatric Association (1989/1990) and director of the National Institute of Mental Health (1978–1984), Dr. Pardes remains an outspoken advocate for the homeless mentally ill and has continually lobbied for social service programs to benefit this neglected group. He has written numerous articles on the condition of mental health care in the United States and has recommended that the problems of the homeless be addressed during medical residence training. In his presidential address to the APA, he called on psychiatrists to "defend human values."

ROBERT W. RIEBER is professor of psychology at the John Jay College of Criminal Justice and the Graduate Center of the City University of New York. He also serves on the faculty of the Psychiatry Department at Columbia University's College of Physicians and Surgeons. Dr. Rieber has edited close to two dozen works in the fields of psychology, linguistics, and criminal justice. He is the founder and editor of the *Journal of Communication Disorders, Journal of Psycholin-*

guistic Research, and *Journal of Social Distress and the Homeless*. He has taught at Rutgers and Pace universities and is the author of a current book, *The Psychopathy of Everyday Life and the Institutionalization of Stress*. He is a fellow of the New York Academy of Sciences, the American Association for the Advancement of Science, and the American Anthropological Association. Throughout his career, he has been concerned with the integration of the capabilities of the human organism to assimilate, organize, and communicate information.

MEL ROSENTHAL is a photographer and teacher. His particular concern is the relationship between changing social conditions and their influence on individuals. He is best known for his work that documents the life of a land rescue community in Puerto Rico, *Villa Sin Miedo Presente!* (Claves Latinoamericano, Mexico), and his book *The South Bronx of America* (Curbstone Press, Ct.). His photographs of Costa Rica, Puerto Rico, Cuba, Nicaragua, Vietnam, and Mexico and of the crises in homelessness and health care in New York City have appeared in books, magazines, newspapers, and exhibitions throughout the world. He is represented by Impact Visuals and directs the photography programs in New York City at Empire State College, which is a part of the State University of New York system.

PETER H. ROSSI is the Stuart A. Rice Professor of Sociology and the director of the Social and Demographic Research Institute at the University of Massachusetts, Amherst. He is also the co-editor of *Social Science Research*. Dr. Rossi has served as director of the University of Chicago's National Opinion Research Center and as a professor of sociology at both Harvard and Columbia universities. He has received numerous awards for his work, including the Commonwealth Award for Career Contributions to Sociology and the Donald Campbell Award for Outstanding Methodological Innovation in Public Policy Studies. He is the author of many books, which include *The Politics of Urban Renewal* and *Reforming Public Welfare*. His most recent works are *Without Shelter: Homelessness in the 1980's* and *Down and Out in America: The Origins of Homelessness*. A product of the depression era himself, Dr. Rossi has long been concerned with national social problems, urban poverty, and public policy.